GREEN REIGN

LEADERSHIP

"Business Lessons To Ensure Leadership Dominance"

PETER WEEDFALD

President

GEN ONE VENTURES

WWW.GENONEVENTURES.COM

ISBN: 0615573282
ISBN 13: 9780615573281

ACKNOWLEDGEMENT

For my wonderful dedicated wife FrancesAnn and my smart, caring daughter Tara Lynn who supported me in running and playing through many rough and tumble, happy years of business leadership.

CONTENTS

BE FORWARD
by Al Berrios

You are never too old to set another goal or to dream a new dream.

C.S. Lewis (1898–1963)

Peter Weedfald was honored to present Green Reign Leadership principles at Baruch College in New York City.

I asked Peter Weedfald, senior vice president of sales, marketing, and operations for Samsung Electronics, to break away from his long business days to deliver a keynote presentation to teachers, students, and local business leaders at Baruch College in New York City. Peter stepped out of his intense business role to share his experience with those interested in understanding the heavy grind and potential opportunities of business leadership. It was cool for the students, who roared with laughter, and Peter was much funnier, in an intimidating, *Sopranos* kind of way, than the last time I had heard him speak. I thought about all the potential business opportunities that could result from this amazing event, from Peter's vision and tactical support for Baruch College students and teachers, and from his docent approach in delivering the dignity of knowledge for those hungry for success. As president of Al Berrios & Company, a leading marketing and consulting firm in New York, I was proud to experience Peter's jaunty and caring spirit and his top-of-the-game leadership approach.

He talked about his approach to sales and marketing leadership, his views on competition, and his aggressive approach with the software tool called customer relationship management (CRM), to ensure customer intimacy always comes first. Peter defines the acronym as "customers really matter." Peter's own career goals were clear, even at his level as senior vice president of sales, marketing, and operations for Samsung Electronics and as Samsung's chief marketing officer for North America. I've watched and learned from his leadership policies on employees, customers, and competitive brand relations in his six divisions across North America and from his humble, yet righteous dedication to all the communities that Samsung serves. Peter's muscular use of the English language strikes fear into listeners; he's a hyper-educated, ankle-gnawing, fist-throwing, cut-throat competitor. He's arrogant in his knowledge of his (and your) business, yet disarmingly congenial. Students and teachers loved it. Younger executives in the audience admired it. Experienced executives found it vulgar but respected it. Everyone knew Samsung, and now they were meeting the guy running sales, marketing, and operations who was responsible for their knowing it. Since

Peter's been at his position, Samsung has increased the value of its brand to just slightly below Sony's, according to *Business Week*'s InterBrand annual rankings - a huge accomplishment for a brand previously considered cheap, and a testimony to his ability. In fact, during Peter's tenure, he and the Spartan team he led helped to make Samsung Electronics into the fastest-growing brand five years in a row according to this same InterBrand study. Incredible new Samsung digital electronic products combined with smart, highly competitive brand and sales activities created positive, market-changing results for the company. Under Peter's leadership, Samsung Electronics, North America dramatically grew its leadership position in sales from $350 million in consumer electronics sales to a whopping $3.5 billion by the time he resigned from the company. Samsung Electronics USA garnered the number one competitive product market share position in all four categories of television technologies under Peter's local leadership: LCD, plasma, DLP, and CRT Slim Fit television formats.

Peter has no qualms about being direct. He doesn't give interviews to trade publications because he doesn't believe company secrets should be given out for competitors to exploit. If competitors observe his strategy rather than pontificating about their plans, they might stand a chance against him and his team members. But at his level, competitors are also partners, so their mistakes benefit him and may also directly affect his kinetic Samsung strategy.

During his presentation, Peter didn't advocate any strategy or medium (although he had some pretty convincing arguments for a couple that he discussed). Instead, he opened our minds to "choice, not chance." He empowered the audience like he does his customers each day through his competitively smart, sharp, and ambient business strategy.

Success lies in consumer choice (a concept I've personally advocated since I founded Al Berrios & Company), and Samsung is proving it. Peter said it more eloquently, though, by reminding us that "brand is the refuge of the ignorant" and that marketers face a balancing act when offering consumers a choice between consistency and complexity in products. But the key is always research and plan choices for consumers and channel partners. We all like a choice between a course of action and its relevant alternatives to solve our problems and to carry out our dreams.

Peter opened up another fascinating can of worms. His perception of ad agencies and media companies is drastically different from what you would expect to read about in a trade publication. In his presentation, he acknowledged their value and usefulness, but explained why they weren't always relevant based upon either individual business experience or lack of, for everything he needed to accomplish in his strategy: an explanation that advertising and media companies don't generally agree with for fear of irrelevancy. Reading advertising trade publications regarding agency success simply gives you the nice pat-on-the-back version of the industry. Winning advertising awards means little if your product and brand sales do not explode positively. Business reality is many times far afoot from such accolades, particularly when dealing with powerful executives and a Board of Directors who demand high competitive performance throughput, from their expensive marketing investments.

Peter is reminiscent of executives like C. J. Fraleigh at General Motors, Steve Heyer at Coca-Cola, and James Stengel at Proctor & Gamble. These executives remind the sales, marketing, and leadership world that their advertising buying power doesn't give leadership a reason to consolidate and negotiate better with them. In fact, they don't care as long as we give them the opportunity to reach their customers at a reasonable price. (If you think about the implications and opportunities of this, then you pretty much understand what executive leaders at Peter's level generally think about the current ad agency and media establishment.) There were representatives of many big, formidable companies in attendance for Peter's talk, which was intended to be an academic discussion aimed at younger, curious minds about strategy, sales and marketing within any global marketplace. Well done Peter, really well done. Please work even harder to help educate and lead our children into fertile, fruitful careers and opportunities for a lifetime.

Peter Weedfald presenting to young minds, teachers and New York business leaders at Baruch College. This opportunity to engage was created by a very smart, caring business leader, Al Berrios (also pictured on stage).

LEADERS ARE FORWARD

Believe you can and you're halfway there.

Theodore Roosevelt (1858–1919)

For me personally, there is no greater leadership honor than to earn a man's or woman's trust. There is no greater honor than to stand before young, hungry, and ambitious minds who dream of the art of the possible and young people who dream of becoming world-class business leaders. I love to have ambitious, energetic minds question me and challenge my mettle, my experience and tenable viewpoints in building world class opportunities. Leadership is all about well-spent, well-fueled time and correspondence in the arena of creative ideas and disciplined leadership. Leadership is all about the ability to initiate, motivate, and promulgate a team to best deliver on the assets of the business and the expected forecast with individual contributions that together fulfill the stated goals. I am honored and gratified to present my Green Reign Leadership approach to successful business focus, which helps leaders avoid the traps that lead to so many beleaguered, untested business substrates that fail.

It is not easy to present well-written, meaningful words in a book. So many of you have wanted, and frankly have earned the right, to write your own tomes describing your successes and your insights. You might also have a request to offer your vast and keen knowledge and your leadership fortitude. My life, perhaps like yours, has been fast, dauntless, and often furious. My leadership life has been focused on the core points of business: sales, product management, brand marketing, multimodal digital advertising, public relations (PR) communications, supply operations, Internet assets, distribution, profit and loss (P&L) management, and executive operational leadership. My personal life has been focused on, and dedicated to, my wonderful and beloved family: my beautiful wife FrancesAnn and my loving daughter Tara.

I write these words while thinking of how our collective lives have been an instant flash forward and at times a flash backward. This must surely match your own personal experience, your own business mortality. Or perhaps you are just getting started and want—make that demand—the dignity of knowledge and of sales and business leadership, as you muscle up your own leadership constitution through this rough-and-tumble business world we travel together. Words, my reading associates, are simple to type. Actions, as we know, take time and intensity to build and time to protect against bigger and more agile competitors.

I experience great humility in my daily business life. I say, "We are not shrinking violets, but bold summer roses...yet we play our own part in the perennial beds of business, never letting our egos dominate the needs of the garden as a whole." We wish to be mighty business warriors and leaders. You might want to keep this business warrior stuff a secret between us; the unwashed and the uninitiated will not understand.

We who lead and direct strive for perfection in fiduciary protection and leadership excellence. We are as durable as steel in daily disciplines, while allowing others around us to enjoy the glory of our team victories. We experience the pain and humiliation of losses along the sometimes negative path of forecasted and expected growth. We pay a heavy toll to learn and balance wisdoms learned through our hyper-aggressive and disciplined leadership postures. I am so honored that you are reading my words and digesting my thoughts. Thank you for making me a part of your leadership team.

You may be recalling the many "leaders" you have worked for, or work for now—the ones you would be so honored to work with again and the ones you painfully recall, thinking, "No more, please, no more." I have been blessed to have had the "lucky leadership eight" in my business career: seven caring and sharing mentors whom I have learned from along the way. Eight I embrace forever, with a grateful heart. I continue to be lost in admiration for their urbane leadership; their great, caring hearts; their canny dedication, and their trust in me and in those they served along the way. All their teaching can be boiled down to one sentence: "If you want to be the leader, act like the leader."

Each of my lucky eight is also known as tenable market makers and competitive juggernauts. It was my great fortune to work, learn, and run fast at their sides. My mentors have included Howard Wood from Lanier Business Systems, Sam Huey from the Ziff Davis Publishing Corporation, Al DiGuido from BigFoot Interactive, James Chu from the ViewSonic Corporation, Dong Jing Oh from Samsung Electronics, Marc Bertino from General Electric and Jeffrey Huang from Bionime Corporation. I add my family, including my lovely partner and wife for life, FrancesAnn, and my incredible and dynamic daughter, Tara, as mentor eight. In business we must provide a profit for our company or we are fired, and that is true at home as well. You must also provide a moral and dollar profit for your family's lifestyle or you will hear the immortal words in your backyard or living room from your wife or your family: "You're fired."

You each have your own favorite leaders and mentors. You also have scars from painful leadership experiences along the way. I have always said, "Take the great assets from your best leadership mentors and slip these into your growing selection of wisdom." Take the worst leaders you had—the "it's all about me, me, me" sad sacks you endured—and ensure you never, ever inflict their poor habits, lack of selling and leadership prowess, or lack of care for others' personal success on another human being. *Place those poor experiences into your torn pockets so they will easily fall away. That's where they belong.*

INTRODUCTION
TO GREEN REIGN

How poor are they that have not patience.

Shakespeare (1564–1616)

Peter Weedfald was honored to present Green Reign Leadership principles at Farleigh Dickinson University's Silverman College of Business. The presentation was within and part of the Rothman Institute of Entrepreneurship.

Why did I choose *Green Reign* as the title for a doctrine I profess as a leadership necessity? *Green*, as we well know, is a positive and uplifting word, color, and symbol, which ties in well with a global leadership foundation, especially considering Mother Earth herself is green. Of course, we wait impatiently for a traffic light to turn green so we may move forward. Our money, the symbol and instrument for building and expanding global leadership success, is also green. In C-level hallways, the budgets and forecasts are focused on positive green attainment, not red-ink losses. Actors are offstage in a green room to relax and reenergize before they go on air in front of millions of people. Green seems to be the most positive color in our personal and business lives and denotes expectations for success and happiness.

Reign, as you know, is the dominating power or influence of leadership. It is also the period of time a specific leadership will prevail. It can attest to or arrest a questionable remedy and ensure that righteous discipline is enjoyed by all.

Green Reign is about positive, everlasting, and fruitful power; command, in the language of great leadership. It's leadership that does not bark or bite, but rather encourages and guides a person, an organization, or an entire enterprise into herculean efforts. Green Reign is all about winning a tough competitive journey. I do not know anyone who does not want to win. I do, however, know many smart leaders who want to be mentors under the wide, sheltering umbrella of Green Reign Leadership. We all want to win—in sports, in love, in business—and we want to win in our ability to motivate a team in every opportunity within our business lives. *Winning is everything, losing is nothing.*

Green Reign Leadership explores the art of leadership excellence across a variety of business disciplines and the logic of fiscal responsibility and measurement. The book is not a standard step-by-step leadership method of knowledge build, but rather it is designed to allow the reader to navigate through any chapter on leadership thoughts and principles as needed. Green Reign Leadership is a guide to varying business areas: it is a friend to those who desire greater results, smarter leadership initiatives, and a different path to team success. We will reveal the inner passion of leadership sometimes hidden, sometimes already pumping and stirring within, but sometimes missing in would-be, could-be, or should-be business leaders. But first we'll explore some fun, keen observations from a lifetime of leadership dedication.

Green Reign Leadership also applauds many business leaders who we are honored to have engaged with, to run with through our business lives. Sometimes they are our peers, sometimes our reports, sometimes outside partners and sometimes even those who we report to. I am constantly reminded of the incredible birr, discipline and dedication of so many I have been honored to run with over the years. So many I have shared with, learned from, won and lost with: so many who have cared about my success as I have cared about their personal success. They are smart, dedicated, personal demanding, unyielding, dauntless and incredible market competitors. Learn and earn from their business leadership, from their passion to find the fissure of opportunity in the competitive granite wall, reflect on just what motivates them, what elevates them above the din of fierce and hungry competitors. Green Reign Leadership is highly focused on the purpose of educating our children, ourselves, team members and sometimes even those we report to. Always with ego parked at the door, always with a caring and mindful determination to unite, to focus the fight against our competitors as we muscle up our intentions and capabilities as one united leadership team.

Speaking of dedication, I dedicate this book to my incredibly creative, beautiful, and smart wife, FrancesAnn Weedfald, and to my young, determined, and adored daughter, TaraLynn Weedfald. As I have traveled across the world for decades on a multitude of silver bullets at thirty-five thousand feet, through cloudy, windy sometimes sunny skies it is my FrancesAnn and TaraLynn who kept me warm, my heart pumping, and my resolve strong. God bless them, both; God bless us all.

1

GREEN REIGN
LEADERSHIP

Whenever you do a thing, act as if all of the world were watching.

Thomas Jefferson (1743–1826)

Here is a bold statement to consider: *All of life is a sale*. A sale will be made today: either you will sell me on an idea, goods, or services, or I will sell you. In fact there is a passage in the Bible, James 4:2 which reads, "You receive not because you ask not." All sales opportunities, frankly even most simple conversations begin with a proposition and should end with a variety of closing questions, such as, "do you agree?" or "may I go ahead and place your order?" Proficiency in selling and marketing should be a standard bill of fare for all executive leadership, within any discipline or role as well as for all parts and aspects of our personal and business lives.

By the way, it is true that you should "never let them see you coming." In a sales exchange, language such as "I am going to *pitch you* on purchasing this product" needs to be replaced with "I am going to *present you* this product for your consideration." The word *pitch* reeks with low class and near arrogance within a sales process. Worse yet, you immediately alert the prospect of your intention to sell hard. You set up instant resistance and immediately pit your intentions against a prospect who's been alerted to take a bulwark stance against your very good efforts. Not convinced? Which phrase is more inviting to you at home or at business: "I have a *present* for you," or "I have a *pitch* for you?" Which phrase lets prospects see you coming and allows them to set up their granite wall of defense?

The problem is if your senior leader—let's say your president—has spent his or her entire life in engineering. He or she may not be attuned to the language of selling products, selling through the assets of advertising and product management, selling partnerships, selling Wall Street analysts, or selling the entire company and family of team members. Of course, it is not the leader's fault: your leader was promoted for excellence in the engineering field. He or she inspired others in engineering to greatness.

As much as this particular engineering leader inspires his or her teams through engagement, he or she quietly, secretly keeps the deep secret: "I do not know if my EVP of sales or CMO, or CTO, or CFO, or CIO is a winner, as I do not have those disciplines. I do not even have interest in the subject matter." In addition, within our new world order of digital weapons and assets, a multitude of men and women at the top do not understand these varying subjects. This means they cannot marshal relevant decisions on the current economy or build platforms of assets.

Think I am kidding? Think of yourself, flexing your business muscles as you rise in the enterprise. Think of yourself as an epic leader preparing to shred the rule books of business and establish a Green Reign Leadership strategy to subjugate a competitor or two. Think how few leaders really understand or are equipped to know what an organization should be deploying, monitoring, aggregating, mining, pushing, and pulling through the instant nanosecond weapon of choice—the Internet. Of course the CEO relies on others; however, the point is that it takes subject matter experts at the very top of the organization to lead the strategy through the Internet across varying company assets to ensure a competitive advantage.

Speed, as I declare often, is leadership's most profitable friend: "increases in productivity deliver increases in profitability," especially on the digital asset side of the business. Canny leadership coupled with hyper-speed create the opportunity to best compete on a global scale.

So now here is the humble yet aggressive leadership benediction and foundation we collectively attempt to live by:

The Green Reign Leadership Doctrine:

We are not oracles, we are not autocrats, and we are not viceroys. Our sagacity and vision are only knee-deep in a vast, highly competitive, and hyper-changing digital business world. We have been honored to work for great men and women and build great teams of disciplined people and future leaders. We spend our entire lives acting like leaders so that we can become great leaders. We are proud of our focus and our leadership across all areas of the business, designed to strengthen our future leadership roles and responsibilities.

We are not sure just when we will be considered business leaders. We do want everyone to know the intense leadership sobriety we bring to our teams every day, to ensure we will succeed and will never be shackled in ignorance through our business journeys. Our intense business focus allows us to personally prepare for the greater role and responsibilities of companywide leadership.

We acknowledge we exist in the cold and unforgiving environment of the profit-and-loss statement. This is what we do for a living, working together across every desktop, every workgroup, and throughout the entire enterprise. We also stand firm as we study, learn, teach, and lead. This is the only way for Green Reign leaders. In our business world, we are as durable as steel, and morally obligated to seek out and deliver expected company decisions.

We acknowledge we live for truth, justice, and rewards for our families. We live to ensure that those who stand with us, next to us, below us, and above us not only have the dignity of business knowledge with fluid communications, but also understand the truth, and recognize the reality, the dangers, the opportunity, and the expected rewards for our success and for our leadership victories."

I am honored to meet your hungry and disciplined eyes. We all seek the mighty grail of opportunity through vast, unexpected competitive gauntlets. I know that we all seek the opportunity to succeed alongside great team members with like minds, pounding and caring hearts, and highly competitive discipline and focus. Together we create the great bastion of fortune for ourselves, our team members, our stock and equity holders, and our wonderful families. This personal demand to achieve is not for the faint of heart or the clock-watchers.

To sum it up, we work daily to uphold our dedication, education, articulation, caring navigation, and competitive subjugation to ensure success for all. It is energizing to read these rhyming words that mirror your own business DNA, which match your leadership instinct for discipline and rewarded dedication.

2

LEADERSHIP DELIVERS CUSTOMER CARE

A man wrapped up in himself makes a very small bundle.

Benjamin Franklin (1706–1790)

I began my sales and marketing career as a salesman for Lanier Business Systems pounding across sunny and cloudy pavement in New York City. It was a lonely, hard knocks position yet an important opportunity in my early days of business that allowed me to learn about myself. There was no base salary, no expenses paid for travel or customer dinners, only a draw-versus-potential sales commission program. At that time, this very rough-and-tumble selling environment caused the turnover of sales people at Lanier Business Systems to exceed 80 percent per year based on failing to sell, failing to recognize how to compete, failing to reach territories' budgeted forecast. This opportunity was not easy, but it built my durable-as-steel leadership foundation. Nothing was tougher than returning each and every day to a sales office at 6:30 p.m. after knocking on doors for ten hours and declaring to your sales peers, "Today I sold nothing." Nothing was so gratifying than to declare on your successful days on the street to those same sales peers and management, "I sold $18,000 worth of word processors today."

I learned humility, I learned the horror and pain of constant personal rejection, I learned to study, appreciate and engage with those around me who knew how to gain success, who found, commanded and lead others through the successful pylon of sales and marketing leadership. For all of this pain and eventual gain, I am so personally fortunate yet saddened for those in life who have not experienced the same rough and tumble road to achievement, towards building their own personal leadership foundation.

My ten years of highly successful, hard-core selling and marketing with Lanier Business Systems granted me promotions and incredible leadership roles. Each position both honored and armed me with sales, marketing and operational knowledge and fortitude. I learned that brand—my brand, a company brand, a product brand—is a promise.

And the very best leadership brands deliver on that promise better and smarter than their direct competitors each and every day. Brands also have a multitude of customer touch points away from corporate headquarters: the products themselves, the service center, the advertising and customer heroes employed to ensure best customer experiences, best returns on brand promise. It is the responsibility of an organization's leadership to ensure the brand experience is highly valued, tuned for best performance, and is better than any competitors' brand performance. Controlling and commanding these touch points to ensure such brand leadership is no easy task. This challenge, call it this brand opportunity, can be either a competitive threat if weak or a competitive weapon of choice when strong and well articulated to your employees and your customers.

Green Reign Leadership is all about your personal brand, your company brand leadership. The book is about the central importance of a leader's brand attributes and how they affect the entire company's brand that is connected through products, services, partnerships, distribution right into the living rooms, retail locations, and the boardrooms of potential customers. Any business leader's brand must begin with a demanding and keen eye for customer excellence and profitable customer relationships. Many leaders profess that they are customer centric, yet over time it is revealed that their talk is nothing more than management blather—the right thing to say. Customer centricity should be any leader's or company's greatest competitive brand advantage. It is at the core of the difference between weakness and kindness in building a world-class leadership brand, a world-class organization.

True customer care, centricity, and focus is all about brand and leadership kindness. If you care about every aspect of your company translated and exposed through products, through your brand value, then over time you will be able to ask for a few more pennies for your products and brand. Hence, kindness and care for customers will be rewarded through profitability over time. Weakness, on the other hand, is the cold, dormant mechanical flash of advertising through various mediums, such as a pretty product brochure, or an Internet or TV advertisement. Kindness is having a viable warranty program with enough customer service representatives. Kindness is having highly trained retail sales people who really care about customers' buying experiences. Kindness is answering your phone and emails with honesty and gratefulness when a customer calls to buy or even to complain; both offer an opportunity to ensure greater brand value based on your caring leadership response.

As leaders, we must never mistake or accept weakness for kindness within your organization or within your perceived brand value—your financial brand equity. Weakness is always an opportunity to improve. However, weakness can also be an advantage that you sadly hand to your competitors as they command smarter brand recognition and customer kindness through each and every touch point of their organization. To best recognize, respond to, and crush brand and organizational weakness, Green

Reign Leadership offers these four customer relationship mistakes to avoid:

1. A silent refusal to be flexible with your business relationships to match each of your customer's expectations and styles of engagement.
2. Misplaced weakness and lack of understanding in how to gain new business, not realizing or acknowledging your sales and marketing teams simply did not "earn the right" to ask for the business while your competition did.
3. A series of brand and product "fat claims" through your advertising, sales presentations, and marketing programs that your company or your brand does not pay off—the inability to impress customers through leadership kindness defined here as genuine and relevant organizational customer experience of excellence.
4. The kinetic failure to listen and respond to customer requests, problems, and opportunities with caring kindness, relevancy, and speed.

Many years ago when I competed on the streets of New York City, I realized through customer engagements that it was never good enough to simply offer better, featured products with more aggressive pricing. It was never good enough to just deliver the products on time or proclaim our great advertising and marketing programs. The winning customer centric formula that worked again and again beyond better products and services was to be kind and caring to each and every customer.

Believe it or not, I stay in touch with so many customers and company team members because they are kind to me and stay in touch even if we no longer do business together. That is personal brand building, the power of kindness in customer engagements, and my former customers mirroring leadership back to me. The best part is I know their kindness for my brand, our wonderful relationship makes them also feel good, and extends their brand kindness inside and outside their building for their customers. As I like to say, as a leader, never misunderstand kindness for weakness. Without customer kindness, your personal brand, your team members' results, and your company's future potential will be weakened by those competitors who lead with better products, more caring services, and genuine, highly competitive customer kindness. Leadership defines customer relationships. Green Reign Leadership defines the need for the most formidable customer care, customer kindness to ensure your greatest competitive advantage, and your greatest brand value.

3

THE WONDER AND THUNDER OF LEADERSHIP

He speaks but says nothing.

Shakespeare (1564 – 1616)

As we begin our Green Reign Leadership journey I believe it is important to best define the attributes and best of breed core business engines of superior leadership. To recognize smart, dedicated and caring leadership to ensure we appreciate and potentially duplicate those merits and attributes as we grow and take on more responsibility, more team members to nourish, to grow, to protect and mentor.

I believe all of us at one time or another had been pachyderms. We were sensitive to our raw feelings and emotions, improvising our defensive response and reactions unnaturally, unhappily. Frankly, we should be appreciative for those "leaders" past who ridiculed us, those who caprice our early brave resolve, for those who unwittingly made us sharper, thicker skinned, strengthened our personal mettle and reversed our defense. The best of us reengineered solicitously against the din of poor leadership evolving into "can do, will do, done" offense mode. **World class leaders are defined, measured and graded through their protractions, their actions, their reactions, their contractions and their natural, formidable attraction.** Superior, proven and trusted leadership is also powered by kinetic, highly relevant learning's and improvisations based on experience, based upon crisp critical thinking, business judgment and sales motivation.

If you polarize a supply chain array of disciplined and focused leadership under the ribs of clear strategy, tactics and courses of action, you will reveal and can juxtapose the substrate of their business DNA; the fabric of their commitment, the speed and agility of their capabilities. Leaderships polarized commitment and capability chain links measure, metric and medium whether the leader is: **De-active – Inactive – Reactive – Active – Pro-active – Hyper-active – Super Active.** In each case and or as aggregated together, the ability to steer and merit success, to act offensively regarding opportunities is as important as digging in defensively regarding threats in competitive share, changing market conditions. Great leaders are created, not born. Superb leaders, highly effective leaders, self develop, self medicate with knowledge to docent themselves through a never ending thread of self regulated study, relevant education, training and applied experiences. **It is the Wonder of superior leadership that augers and creates the Thunder of orchestrated victories.**

Peter Weedfald delivers the Wonder and Thunder of Green Reign Leadership.

Having said this, we attempt to gain consensus by defining leadership as: **the ability to influence, stimulate and energize others to focus on and accomplish a greater goal.** Highly effective leader's story, plan, influence, energize and upgrade the common goal, into the demanded dream of one team. The lucent report card of leadership is best graded by the caliber and business judgment of followers, by the ability and measured results of said greater goal. While the influence of intelligent leadership is best fueled by moral and royal values, trust worthiness, ethics, character and the spirit of generosity, it is the smart knowledge of leadership that grounds united logic for the team, commonplaces clear determination to achieve or exceed the goal.

Mature leadership offers three additional important and unique magnetic characteristics versus standard management or simple authority: **inspiration, motivation, communication.** Best of breed leadership aggregates and motivates trust, confidence and the demand engine for Spartan followers to become the same or to aspire to a heightened notch above greatness when learned, when earned. For those who personally demand to become a leader, I suggest you follow this business benediction I have professed for two decades: **"If you want to be the leader, act like the leader."** Just make sure you are learning from and following the right leader, to act like the leader you wish to someday become.

Of course management and leadership vary greatly. Think of management as the position of an assigned boss designated to deliver results while leadership is the role designed to focus on and achieve the highest possible goals, together. Think of leadership in the language of honorable business and moral character coupled with selfless service and support for the organization, for the team. Think of leadership responsibility as a guiding light, respected and warranted by followers who demand a greater sense of purpose and direction, who wish to learn and competitively achieve higher ground. Team members want to respect, hold and duplicate fond and refulgent leadership. To perhaps one day earn the right to become the leader; they themselves. To ensure we fulfill our responsibilities to teach, train, inspire and build future global leaders I offer 11 Green Reign Leadership guiding principles to build, mature and orchestrate an army of highly effective business leaders for today and tomorrow:

1. **Deliver trust, offer confidence and commanding capabilities for your team members.**
2. **Preach, teach and unleash your overall business strategy to your team.**
3. **Openly and consistently reveal fiduciary progress or lack of achievement with respect to targeted goals individually and companywide.**
4. **Help each employee define and road map how they can personally contribute to the goals from both a pecuniary standpoint and with respect to team engagements.**
5. **Communicate often and always across all viable channels.**

6. **Reveal, promulgate and portend a competitive, fun cultural spirit of determination.**
7. **Be actionable, be measurable, be accessible, not just professorial.**
8. **Know your team members history; help plan the dream of their future.**
9. **Ensure through your personal leadership to always unleash capacity, never punish productivity.**
10. **Learn and earn to deliver and share the dignity of knowledge with your team, the spoils of financial success with your entire organization.**
11. **Focus leadership on your customers and they in turn will focus profitable, long term leadership on you.**

Great leadership inspires team greatness. Great leadership challenges the process, challenges the strategy, and challenges the team to inspire victorious results. Great leadership utilizes superior business judgment, critical thinking and team motivation to steer around competitive business remoras, competitive advantage. Inspire others, enable others, model others, energize the hearts of others and encourage others to become the leaders they pine to be, to continue their demanding role on the offense, to deny the bulwark distracters they met and feared so many years ago on the defensive side of leadership. And of course, unleash your competitively aggressive business and market offense by unleashing your highly trained and aspiring leadership team members.

The Wonder and Thunder of Green Reign Leadership: Go ahead and create some or get some... or be kind and just get out of the way!

4

APPETENCE FOR THE IMPOSSIBLE

Nothing is so common as the wish to be remarkable.

Shakespeare (1531-1592)

Amazing times.... This is an important time to believe in the art of the impossible in business, government, and on a personal basis. The appetence for determined results can best be articulated by a highly viable and professional sales thread and formidable leadership exchange. If you are not personally vested and trained in professional selling and lack great command of your lexicon, which should be crisp to deliver your point of view, then I suggest your ability to win in business or at home is not tuned for best results; it is not tuned to accomplish the impossible business. Green Reign Leadership believes in the importance and fortitude of selling and marketing excellence as the foundation for superior leadership in any business venture.

And yes, Shakespeare said it best; we all *want to* be remarkable. But we know it takes personal determination to study, practice, and rebound from the wounds of failure to become a highly relevant business leader—a leader who delivers on his or her promise through the art of the deliverable, with competitive vigor, advantage, and resulting benefits. You can ensure such consistent, positive results relevant to the demands and opportunities of your own business and home life if you truly practice the greater command and skills of professional selling and leadership. We are all, in fact, nothing more than carpenters of words. Some "carpenters" *dream* of remarkable deeds while others can actually *move and craft new mountains* of pedestrians to their points of view.

Peter Weedfald selling and marketing the Green Reign Leadership way to over one million people in Times Square, New York City receives a positive and energizing response.

There are a multitude of business, government, and personal examples of energizing and effective leadership. In each and every case, I suggest that individuals prove their greater selling skills by first creating and commanding personal demands to succeed. They can do this by drawing and painting viable disciplines through their determined words and actions. This is professional selling at its best. This thinking breaks the commonality point that Shakespeare articulates so well and grinds against our business and personal egos: there are truly remarkable leaders who have moved from wishing for, to accomplishing the impossible. The real question is just what are we waiting for to carve out our own remarkable accomplishments, not just our own remarkable dreams?

To be remarkable in Business America is no easy task. Competition is fierce, targeting and subjugating market leaders with unbridled optimism and personal demands to succeed. Ignoring the lessons of leadership failures is potentially as dangerous and punishing as losing business itself. Remember, risk never sleeps, competitors never give up, and there is no leadership mission without profitable margins. Teach your team members to lead with their smart minds coupled with highly relevant economy of language. Teach them the habit to win through your selling victories and a disciplined demand to win every day. The great Vince Lombardi said it best when he said: "Winning is a habit...unfortunately so is losing." And we all agree; winning is everything, losing is nothing.

Below are nine principles for successful sales leadership designed to ensure strength in business substrates, engagements, and formidable growth in leading a team to positive and impactful business goals. The words mirror those of leaders who are aplomb in motivating teams to success, inculcating by example and personal toil. In essence, these rules represent the mettle of successful leaders who succeed through their highly effective, highly competitive sales approaches and deliveries.

I have said for many long business days and many rough-and-tumble years that "if you want to be the leader, act like the leader." These fourteen rules are, or should be, the core strength, the ribs of the wide umbrella of senior leadership excellence, leadership expectations, and leadership deliverables to ensure there is always shelter from the competitive storm, a keen focus on attaining business opportunity, and achieving business goals. Remarkable leadership is shared openly and founded within:

1. **Your business judgment—your business disciplines.**
2. **Your critical thinking—your careful listening.**
3. **Your sales motivation—your sales comprehension.**
4. **Your sales capabilities—your sales articulation and navigation.**
5. **Your creativity—your imagination.**
6. **Your heart for the innocent, your personal actions to prove it.**
7. **Your ability to manage objections, handle rejections, and create exceptions.**
8. **Your ability to ask the right questions to then understand and appreciate the right answers.**
9. **Your ability to share, care, teach, protect and project your entire team.**
10. **Your ability to honor, care for and serve your customers the same way you do for your brand, your team, the same as for your friends and family.**
11. **Your astute business relevancy, your ability to articulate the right strategy.**
12. **Your ability to learn every day, to build consensus, to build a team with united, knowledgeable competitive advantage.**
13. **Your care, focus and welfare for your customers, for your team focused opportunities.**
14. **Your ability to identify, attract and retain the very best individual talent to build opportunity and competitive advantage.**

These are Green Reign Leadership market-experienced thoughts specifically from a sales leadership perspective designed for your own personal measurement. These principles are also training subjects for your team members as well as measurement tools for perspective new hires during the interview process.

5

HOW SMART IS YOUR LOGIC?

Logic will get you from A to B. Imagination and creativity will take you everywhere.

Albert Einstein (1879 – 1955)

Green Reign Leadership believes smart logic makes an argument sound while creative business passion makes an argument, a sales presentation or a negotiation sound **logical**. Logic is the engine of your mind, as passion is the engine of your heart. Remember to keep them separated, to never allow your mind to battle your heart and vice versa especially through the "heart" of a negotiation. Instead, mature, control and command the resolve of your passion (heart) and deploy kinetic critical thinking and business judgment through your very sharp and keen logic (mind). Then fold them both in very carefully, very purposively with meaningful and profitable relevancy designed and tuned for the negotiating session. **Through the masterful art of negotiation, it is the further articulation of opportunity through smart,**

relevant and creative passion that earns the right to unite... earns the right to jointly engage in a profitable market making fight.

Sounds esoteric? It's not! Sounds like fun? It is, especially and only if you master and command these two very distinct yet highly complementary business engines and can bespeak your negotiating and selling prowess across the table. Just like baking a magnificent, happy, and delicious and award winning layer cake! The logic of articulating the right ingredients, at the right heating temperature with the right timing requirements in perfect congress delivers award winning logical results. Baking a cake is all about logic. Cutting and sharing large slices of your perfectly baked cake with friends, colleagues and family is what stimulates palatable, savory passion. Based on the logical process, foundation and completion of baking your cake you are able to evoke and frankly command the passion and greater creative participation you originally sought. Always first, the mature and relevant creation of a logic award winning foundation. Then when baked to completion, we add the accelerant called passion to cause and stimulate those across the negotiation table to lean into your side to enjoy together a delicious piece of business cake. Professionally speaking, methodically folding and baking logic and passion into your negotiations delivers and exposes the dream of mutual success and happiness. After all, who wants to argue against sound, mutually beneficial business logic? And just who can run from the passion and dream of a delicious slice of business cake? Especially when the price is right, the logic is sound and the cake is creatively very warm, very delicious.

When you speak in the language of logic and world class creative passion, crea-tive vision, you speak in the language of my good friend Peter Max. (pictured are Peter Max and Peter Weedfald).

By the way, please do not treat folding in the passion ingredi-ent as simply conclusive. Rather, you must take personal respon-sibility to stimulate, aggregate and affiliate creative business passion, layered on top of your hard earned logical substrate, through smart, relevant and mutually profitable advantage. Albert Einstein said it best: **"Imagination is more important than knowledge. For knowledge is limited to all we now know and understand, while imagination embraces the entire world, and all there ever will be to know and understand."** Relevant to our thinking and mindful to the great physicist Albert Einstein, knowledge is logic: imagination is creativity. Don't simply be prepared in negotiation through your knowledge and logic as a subject matter expert. Rather ensure your complete proposition is projected through a stimulating vista of imagination and creativity highly relevant and enveloping to the market you intend to serve. **Creative passion is your best competitive advantage as it super fuels the engines of logical, well proven business opportunities.**

In business, the birr of **emotional capital** congeners logic and passion: into a highly competitive and mutually beneficial quid quo pro advantage. Emotional capital, the impactful duopoly of logic and passion, favors the prepared mind, the energizing creative and passionate articulation of the possible based upon business facts. Emotional capital stimulates and builds long term fair and equitable partnerships because when logic and passion unite and spark between two parties, big, viable and long term businesses are negotiated and built. Coupling business logic to business passion can turn any partnership from provider of standard and sturdy products to creator of competitively advantaged and consumer desired products. In addition, we know from historical results, that consumers are willing to pay a few extra pennies for the burnished feeling of emotional capital. Think Apple, a company thriving by coupling the logic of its highly competitive, integrated product offerings with the passion of its creativity, imagination and dream weaving content. This is just why they are so tough to compete with. This fierce and flinty competitive union of logic and passion deliver consumers the emotional capital to want, to desire, to pay extra for brand and product Apple, again and again and again. **This well baked Apple emotional capital cake delivers brand infatuation to a global market, a formidable weapon of choice few companies have ever been able to achieve. My goodness Mr. Steve Jobs, how heavenly brilliant your vision truly was, truly is!**

So let's now explore the power of logic for the purpose of business negotiations. Decision making logic is woefully under-leveraged by some, yet the foremost business weapon of choice for highly successful others. Internally identifying all aggregated, pertinent options and advantaged opportunities with a keen auger for potential outcomes is hard, but smart work. Illuminating corresponding, complimentary and profitable decision paths designed to strengthen the logic of desirable quid quo pro opportunity is the breakfast, lunch and dinner of business Champions. More advanced "Chess Master" business sharks assign probabilities to opportunities, sometimes in micro seconds across the negotiation table, calculating the likely returns on investment from alternative decision paths. **This is baking the cake of leadership logic: superior and exercised logic at its business best.**

To many times we advance vetted business opportunities through a series of collected projects as opposed to an advanced, over arching strategy foundation based upon ambient logic. Articulating a position of strength through the stems of projects sometimes forces you to negotiate against yourself, causing your potentially continent strategic construct to be bamboozled by your own hand. We always negotiate to win, we are clearly tuned and prone to victory in our daily business lives. However, there can be no significant victory without a formidable and profitable strategy enveloped by the durable steel of advantaged logic. Logic, as your core backbone foundation allows you to unleash capacity, steer and command opportunity and advantage tough negotiations before, during and after the exchange. Once your mind has engulfed and captured your negotiating opponent through the course of your venerable business logic, it is then your further responsibility to broaden the joint opportunity by reigning in a united, prosperous and passionate construct. It is this secondary ingredient of business passion layered on top of your business logic that advantages both you and those you negotiate with into a fairly equitable and profitable partnership. Then, as I mentioned, we fold in creative, relevant and market making passion.

The key to applying competitive advantage across the negotiation table should start and stop with a well tested, well researched and calculated decision tree analysis, prior completed. The dignity of knowledge and the ability to apply smartly should be tested in varying options and potential outcomes through a series of related and weighted decisions. Assigning probabilities and weighing-grading alternative decisions will map out best and most likely predictable results towards ensuring mutual profitable opportunity. Structuring the logical proposition, based on critical research and knowledgeable assessment in preparation for the negotiation is in itself competitive advantage at the table.

To be clear, first advantage and secure your winning hand through smart, sound and calculated logic. Logic is defined as: logic (noun) loj-ik: convincing forcefulness; inexorable truth or persuasiveness: the irresistible logic of the facts. Then immediately, without hesitation, move and position your "logic chess pieces" to obligate weight and complement your earned victory to favor your former opponent by folding in highly relevant passion, expressed through brilliant and market relevant creativity. Once baked, this union of logic and passion should deliver emotional capital for the negotiators, emotional capital for the market you are about to serve. Exercises to perfect the art of irresistible persuasiveness through a foundation of business logic and passion should begin with:

- Carefully identifying and examining all feasible, viable alternatives and opportunities in favor of your stated business strategy. Then cross study the same for the company you will negotiate with as if you would be representing their business, not yours. Audit the found gaps and fissures to your desired goals and outcome followed by preparing your smarter case on the offense with highly relevant proof points and broad based market evidence.

- Auguring and jockeying potential post negotiated outcomes to best pre-focus on variances and road blocks towards achieving your ultimate and desired outcome. As an example, the price you wish to gain for your contracted services through negotiation should be backed with already memorialized and financially tested good, better and best pricing scenarios. Do not treat this basis of choice as pre-packaged backup to handle a pricing objection but rather as a formula to gain traction on the negotiation offense offering "choice not chance" excellence in services, support and pricing based on needs, not based on down trodden negotiating.

- Diagramming in the language of decision tree construction is essential to ensure the value of your logic in business negotiation is equal or accelerates the value of your profitable goals. These smart trees need to calculate and reveal essential demands and outcomes to include 1. Acceptable decisions and situations 2. Investments, costs, expenses and returns 3. Probabilities, revenues, profits and timing.

- Certifying potential financial returns from each permutation, combination and supposition discovered within the decision tree exercise. All costs (real, hidden, potential and expected) along with all income (current, projected, rejected and protracted based on market conditions) from each viable limb of your decision trees.

- Calculating with certainty the good, better and best financial scenarios with 5% positive and or negative certainty.

- Refine, potentially recertify your results and proposition through a logical review both as the negotiator and by simulating your review as the company you plan to negotiate with.

- Creativity and passion in business are the united disciplines to turn opportunities based on sound logic into highly competitive actions and financial results.

- Passion in business is the creative ability to turn logical business options into successful and highly motivated revenues, products, brands and market share.

- **"Creativity is seeing what everyone else has seen, and thinking what no one else has thought." (Albert Einstein)**

- *Passion coupled with relevant logic and highly competitive creative is always the negotiating weapon of choice, the secret sauce in becoming a market maker as opposed to a market follower.*

- *Uniting logic and creative passion should be viewed with an ultimate eye of creating emotional capital at the negotiating table, for the market you intend to unite and serve, together.*

Green Reign Leadership believes it is always time to fold in highly relevant business passion on top of smart business logic to portend new, dynamic approaches to over achieve jointly on negotiated covenants. Creative productivity and action as the ribs of your logical proposition in negotiation will always ensure mutual agreement, mutual growth, and mutual and long term profitability. Remember; first win your case, your opportunity, through logic. Then share the expected victory by orchestrating jointly captured passion to accelerate and muscle up balanced support to over achieve on mutually agreed to goals. Negotiations are not about agreeing to projects but rather enjoying and fueling logical, strategic business opportunities folded onto passionate, creative shoulders to garner the weapon of choice: emotional capital.

Should you bake and fold-in both smart logic and creative passion in every business negotiation? Surely yes, if you always to play to win. How smart is your logic? I believe very smart, based upon your Green Reign Leadership negotiating foundation.

6

THE BEST OPPORTUNITIES LIE IN DANGER

The ultimate measure of a man is not where he stands in moments of comfort and convenience, but where he stands at times of challenge and controversy.

Martin Luther King, Jr. (1929–1968)

Before I approach daring to sell and daring to lead, we need to step back and agree that *the very best opportunities lie in facing danger.* If the very best opportunities did not lie in danger then everything in life and everything in business would thrive and achieve beyond our wildest fiduciary imaginations.

As a student of great authors—make that "literary docents"— I personally read and learn from their nearly free sagacity and intellectual capital as often as possible. As an assiduous student of great, highly successful companies and leaders I also read and learn from them, daily. You will realize and discover from these studies that the most effective, competitive dangerous and respected leaders spend enormous time with their customers, listening, caring for, advising, learning and building a quid quo pro business landscape and jointly beneficial future.

As leaders, we must also recognize and capitalize on new, disruptive and change-focused technologies creating positive cause and effect for the washed, potentially dismal failure for the uninitiated. The advantage in understanding and leashing new technologies is that they can stimulate our leadership minds toward incorporating or creating new business opportunities. Opposing business forces are in constant market battle. Those who are able to articulate and navigate technologies in business for competitive advantage in speed and profit will be rewarded with growth, wealth, and team success.

That was true yesterday and is still true today, as new personal and business hardware and software technologies thunder out of manufacturers' warehouses at dizzying speeds. These words remind us all to stay ahead of the hyper-changing, short-product-life cycles we troll through every day. With economy of language, "If you want to win it, you must be in it." Make no mistake, being at the forefront and steering wheel of the latest information technology (IT) ensures aggressive and profitable competitive business advantages.

Truly, the answers for all business leaders are "out there" among our customers and our competitor's customers we pine for. We need to learn from customers and to submit to their guidance and counsel; we need to grow their businesses to grow our own businesses. This is how Green Reign leaders grow their teams, profits, and competitive advantage: by growing their business strategy through their customers' minds and merits. They constantly ask, "What would our customers believe is the right move? What would they think if we did this? What would they buy and how would they profit from our products, our services, and our determination?" This Green Reign mindset drives rational strategies, as opposed to customer-competing irrational strategies. This Green Reign Leadership structure suggests we will never have a current or potential customer ask us, "Are you my competitor or are you my partner?" Always we partner, always we unite, and always we seek opportunities to grow elbow to elbow with our customers first and foremost in mind and in action. Green Reign Leadership believes: "The best opportunities lie in facing danger; the best opportunities are seldom labeled as such."

Speaking of incredible market and customer leadership, let's think of and explore the global success of Starbucks. Starbucks of course, came up with a unique coffee formula coupling the magical, delicious and customer sought out coffee with thousands of highly social, music-throbbing, free-wireless retail locations across America. And then of course, articulated and delivered across the globe. No other business was building or creating this unique, consumer loved taste and social experience. And to this day, no company seems capable of competing with it. Green Reign Leadership compels us to examine this mammoth and highly successful coffee/social-minded juggernaut competitor. We also pause to celebrate and congratulate Starbuck' vision, their smart and creative leadership, their market success.

Perhaps Starbuck's competitors made it too easy, through their own "no risk" leadership approach. Where were the leaders of the once mighty Maxwell House, Folgers, Chock full o' Nuts, Nescafe, and others while Starbucks built their business? Where was Dunkin Donuts during Starbucks' early progress? Where were the multitude of food stores and coffee vendors as Starbucks marched through the streets of America, France, Germany, and Italy, landing on food store shelves around the world? Were they watching, perhaps even praising this competitor? Did they understand the potential results of this new and powerful business maelstrom that Starbucks created by combining social networking, a unique new style of coffee, and music inside and outside their retail shops? Many competitors I must believe have brand, product and services infatuation for Starbucks. As they should, as we all should as all who desire to lead a market, a brand, a team should attest, respect and learn from.

Please, imagine the internal pain of having brand and product infatuation for a mighty new competitor, watching its mighty market leadership unfold; or perhaps imagine Starbucks' leadership is shrinking your own once-viable market share. This dire business situation of "watching, potentially admiring leaders" should perhaps be titled "Red Reign Leadership." Leaders who are lost in admiration for their advancing competitors are only lazy followers—unless they deploy an immediate "war room" mentality to review, plan, and take action to protect and grow their own business. And unless they are smart enough to lead Green Reign Leadership initiatives ahead of competitors, so that they are the ones that others are chasing and admiring. As we know in business, within the markets we serve, first come the leadership innovators, then come the fast and intrepid copiers, then come the sluggish lazy fools, late to the market, late to the shelf space, late to gaining much needed profits in order to survive, in order to grow.

In the language of Green Reign Leadership, you cannot dare to sell and lead, if you are sitting on a metaphoric park bench watching your sales diminish and your brand evaporate, listening to your own employees praise the company outpacing your brand of coffee. It is not good enough to just observe this miracle. Green Reign Leadership suggests: Study your competitor's strengths to avoid your own business weakness. Study your competitor's weaknesses so you may build new business muscle and protective leadership armor.

It is impossible to dare to lead your team and expect to lead a market if you do not assiduously study the market and research consumer and customer desires and demands, as aggregated against the value propositions of your competitors already enjoying market dominance. Remember, "Respect and know your customers; respect and know your competitors; respect, know and apply your market research, and then you should expect to win, expect to reveal and build the Green Reign Leadership strategy to succeed with complete market knowledge."

Take heed, coffee business leaders: the answers are out there. The message and lesson is simple: "You work for consumers; consumers do not work for you." Remember, consumers do not buy a TV; they buy the dream of watching the Super

Bowl in their living rooms. They buy the dream of watching a pirate movie, the fantasy that they are the actual pirates on the ship, swinging across the ropes with swords in teeth as they lay at their leisure in their bedrooms. Consumers love the dreamy experience of the socially charged Starbucks. Starbucks' consumer dream works. It truly works emotionally, and it works in reality.

Green Reign Leadership professes if you *sell the dream, they will all follow.* Green Rein Leadership knows the prime goal of businesses is to "serve the imagination of consumers and business." When served properly, competitively, and with the highest degree of product cosmetics, usability, service and brand, a business is rewarded with accelerating sales, market share, profitability, and brand value. Think how the following brands and corresponding products serve your own imagination instantly by just stating their names here: Apple, Starbucks, Disney, Coca Cola, Facebook, Amazon, Nike, Google, Samsung, BMW, Verizon, GE and many others that I am sure come to mind.

These companies and brands serve our most sensitive imaginations just through name-brand associations. They provide aggressive forms of stimulating, relevant desire and demand within their product offerings, their brand halo. They each deliver highly competitive and profitable Green Reign Leadership demand for their mammoth global brands, for their products. They each create and build both emotional and physical demand for their brands, products and services. This is Green Reign Leadership at its best.

Each and every aspect of the Starbucks business model above and beyond its five-legged stool of unique coffee, social engagement, music, free Internet, and well-distributed retail locations, should be required study in universities and colleges across the globe. Study should include every aspect and touch point of its unique business model: manufacturing, supply chain, brand and distributor partnerships (like United Airlines, etc.), brand-building without spending mammoth amounts on advertising, the social coffee cult it built under the watchful eyes of market leaders—the once competitively durable coffee brands who were blind to the threat. One full semester for business students, please. One full semester for marketing students, please. One full semester for all accounting and engineering students, please.

7

THE DIGNITY OF KNOWLEDGE

A person, who never made a mistake, never tried anything new.

Albert Einstein (1879–1955)

ere's a relevant question: How is it that the best sports coaches are smart enough to come up with instant on-the-field responses, when their offense is being crushed by the defense? Why don't they wait three years to come up with an effective and meaningful counter strategy to block player number seventeen, whose name happens to be Starbucks? Why is it that coaches create new offensive plays, structures, and strategies minute-by-minute and day-by-day, while still maintaining a strong defense? Why? Because this is how the coach, the team's leader, builds a world-class and successful team franchise. Surely coaches unite the power of knowledge of the game's rules with the knowledge of their next competitor's products/players and the knowledge of their own products/players?

Then they add the courage to lead and the demand to succeed to one competitive team. It should be the same in business, don't you agree?

Great, world-class coaches are assiduous in their research. They study, study, study daily, and then bring in their players and subordinate coaches to study along with them, watching films in both slow and fast motion again and again. Coaches and leaders—highly active coaches and leaders—seek their own weaknesses as much as they seek their strengths. They identify and create opportunities by unleashing capacity in assets while driving hyper-productivity. They never punish productivity for failure, instead they punish their competitors through dominant knowledge, smart teachings, and galvanized team leadership designed to accomplish victory. They learn from and teach their teams by developing and dissecting knowledge; they ensure victory through sharing, caring, and awarding the power of team knowledge.

In fact, the best sports and business coaches also know the very best opportunities lie in facing danger. They dare to *study* their competitors, *sell* their teams on progressive changes, and *lead* their teams. They know they are personally obligated to ensure execution and team success. Green Reign Leadership sits on both the offensive and defensive side of winning. I need to write another book, titled *Truly Green Reign Leaders,* which outlines leadership actions and praises great leaders who have fended off the almost unstoppable offense of a Starbucks, or a Kleenex, or a Nike, or a GE, or an Amazon. While Best Buy should be congratulated and heralded as the mighty, winning consumer electronics retail leader, defeating once mighty maverick, competitors and growing market opportunities. Of course Amazon. com has changed and super-fueled the rules for successful market growth by offering consumers lower prices, the largest seemingly endless global aisle product and brand assortments, the most relevant and desired one-to-one on line consumer engagements with nearly perfect speed of service and delivery.

Other Green Reign Leadership examples to write about, to herald together include Samsung Electronics; of course.

Samsung's massive, several decades long rise in brand and product market share is a leadership study in itself. Samsung represents today mammoth and consistent step by step, product by product, unyielding visionary growth. Results pitted and compared competitively against Sony, Panasonic, Toshiba, and Sharp in consumer electronics (CE); against Nokia, Motorola, and Sony Ericsson in cell phones; and versus so many other competitive manufacturers in semi-conductors, home appliances, personal technologies and so much more proves Samsung Electronics to truly be a global market making, leading industry viceroy.

And while no competitor was looking, the mighty Vizio electronics company gained nearly equal, sometimes tied LCD TV market share to Samsung Electronics in 2010 and 2011, selling more TVs in America using little broad based advertising, and with the lowest sales and operating costs versus their CE industry competitors. Vizio took and captured massive market share and opportunity from the venerable titan industry brands. They crafted and perfected a new and unique competitive model and infrastructure. A multitude of channel, factory, and consumer fans vote with their pocketbooks for the Vizio brand and their growing product family. Why? Because Vizio deserves their confidence, buying power and loyalty based upon the success of their smart business foundation, highly competitive product disciplines and operational excellence, for their smart market strategy and for their personal customer care.

Then there is Noel Lee, CEO and founder of Monster Cable and Monster Corporation. He too, created a dynamic and highly competitive Green Reign Leadership business model. Monster Corporation owns the Monster Cable brand of consumer audio and video cables connecting audio and video components together. The company produces both consumer electronics and personal computer accessories, including audio and video cables, headphones, speakers, remotes, and power conditioning accessories. Noel's sagacity, many will agree, allows him to envision and create a better consumer dream and reality for the best video and audio experiences using complementary product lines. The Monster brand and its corresponding product offerings gained maverick market share using social and channel recommendations, higher quality products, and great packaging, not through tired, conventional marketing and advertising wisdom. Monster's results over the years truly mirror Monster's brand name, brand mettle, and consumer brand value. Noel Lee's urbane and very smart leadership will be and should be studied and heralded for many decades to come.

Trust me, the jet stream of frustration in competitive camps is wide, smoky, and obsessed in trying to find the right, long term Green Reign Leadership solution to fight and disarm such formidable brands, products, and service-selling, consumer desired global machines.

We all can cite a multitude of lucent Green Reign Leadership companies that have beaten the odds of behemoth competitors. We can also cite the names of those who lead their teams, viceroys who dared to sell, dared to lead. We must always learn from them and apply their strength and leadership merits to our focused determination, to compare to our own successes, to our own failures.

So, we imagine we can hear in the hallways:

"Hello, sir. We better start articulating demand for our Coffee's Best product lines." "Why is that Mortimer?" the confident executive asks. "I don't really understand, sir, but it's something about a new coffee brand called Starbucks? The leader is some sort of a harbinger, predicting he is going to have six or seven thousand Starbuck's retail locations to serve coffee, designed to bring in happy people, to play music, to deliver free Internet access across the globe. In essence, all designed to best serve consumer imagination." The boss says, "Whoops, too late to respond, but not to worry, Mortimer, we can all now enjoy a 'ioca, mocha, toca, we-r-da-losers' coffee from Starbucks each morning on the way to work here at Coffee's Best. Life is good, Mortimer, as we will drink, spend, surf the Internet, socialize, and enjoy Starbucks coffee every day to best study and understand this cool new coffee character."

"Well, sir, perhaps you're right. I am just afraid they will eat our lunch while we drink their coffee." "Nonsense," says the boss.

"Mortimer, life is good. We will eat their lunch and their delicious deserts nearly every day, along with drinking their coffee and enjoying their music. Remember, they are only one mile from our office building." After listening to these limp-wristed words and observing the wobbly legs of the big boss, he decides that perhaps the new title for the mighty Trojan horse should be the "Starbuck horse." Whoops, too late. The company has already been reclassified as "The Starbuck Juggernauts, with no horsing around, taking no competitive prisoners."

Let us surely learn from maverick business leaders, from successful and failed companies and their team organizations. This is the way to earn our own Green Reign Leadership successes: by studying others, examining and respecting their wins and losses, and navigating our own organizations based on our examination of others who have won and lost in the battle of business. Remember, knowledge should be your primary weapon of choice, a competitive advantage designed to disrupt your competitors. The crisp dignity of knowledge creates market advantage when united with keen product development leadership focused on just how to capitalize through multi-modal product efficiencies and featured superiority in the language of building and or fulfilling consumer demand.

8

SO, LET'S TALK ABOUT GREEN REIGN LEADERSHIP

Once you learn to quit, it becomes a habit.

Vince Lombardi (1913–1970)

et's talk about daring to sell and daring to lead and the eight golden rules of Green Reign **Leadership** that are aimed at building a broad-spectrum business offense with a granite wall-like defense.

The business offense must address the principles expressed as we understand them: create, stimulate, never duplicate, and drive big and wide to eradicate formidable competitors. The defense must adhere to our Green Reign Leadership doctrine wisdom. To accomplish this, study outside forces daily; maintain relentless focus, discipline, and drive to stimulate profitable advancements; be highly creative; and keep your eyes on the rear-view mirror. Develop fluid communications and hire your leadership heroes. Build, create, build again, and create again and

41

again. Make course corrections. Take no prisoners. Only heroes may apply. Most importantly, the team's strategic plan must be sharply focused on increasing asset productivity, which will absolutely increase asset profitability.

I have not had breakfast or lunch during any business day for more than twenty-five years. Yes that's correct: more than twenty-five years. I know we are all very different in heart, body, mind, tolerance, and food requirements. For my own over-pressured body and mind, dancing through a daily torrent of rough-and-tumble selling competitors, daily rejection, and some-times, weekly failures, food was once my reward; even though I knew food slowed me down.

If I eat breakfast or a luxurious business lunch (which I con-sistently did in my early days, because food is a sales warrior's best friend and reward, especially when rejection runs rampant and sales dry up) I get tired, lose my energy, and reduce my jaunty selling spirit. I used food, plenty of food, as a misguided reward for my humbled, rejected, and frightened body and mind, a security blanket that never solved or resolved fruitless selling. It always drugged my mind with fast injections of instant gratifi-cation, instant rewards for my failures, for my disappointments.

Tired, off your game, dragging your feet up and down stairs, knocking on strangers' doors trying to sell something when all you really want to do is sleep off the big lunch you just slammed down in ten minutes. This food-tired business stupor is the worst physical feeling I have ever experienced. Trust me, I learned this food exhaustion lesson when I was twenty-six years old, and have stayed the course of one meal a day ever since. One normal meal a day, eating like a gentleman at a slow-paced dinner, is my reward for long hours and hard work—win, lose, or draw.

Of course we are all built differently and you may need three-plus meals a day to ensure your intensity and competitive advan-tage. As my old boss, the great Mr. D. J. Oh, CEO of Samsung Electronics in North America, used to say to me, "Please, con-tinue." He meant, "Peter, if it works for you and the team to gain market share advantage, please, continue." My own body and mind sell and lead best when I am running on empty and working out intensely in the gym three times a week, focused on the opportunity to win, not on the false reward and security blanket of food.

Well, let's get back to the subject matter: Green Reign Leadership. We cannot define or find ways to favor our leadership capabilities without engaging the digital assets that our competitors and we use. The reason to discuss the following business economies is that each characteristic can harm or benefit our business and leadership success.

Over the past several decades, we have traveled through varying new economies that are shaping the future for generations to come. In the '70s and early '80s a new global economy emerged called the "information economy." The advent of the personal computer put internal business and personal data instantly at our fingertips. Business roared ahead, at least the kind that harnessed and commanded these new business tools. We next traveled through the "knowledge economy," which the global power of the Internet brought on, allowing for instant communications worldwide.

The Internet, I like to say, is "Darwin on speed." It is the fastest union of push and pull through the known galaxy. For consumers, the Internet is faster than a speeding bullet or light itself. We can push out and sell in Paris, France, and pull back the sale from the same European location in a nanosecond; hence, the title "knowledge economy." Indeed, business was changed forever when brick-and-mortar retailers were supplanted by "dot-com commandos" hidden in a cloud of low-cost, hyper-fast competitive brilliance.

Some call the knowledge economy the "me economy," because as consumers trained their fingers and minds to steer around advertising claims, high prices, poor service, time and cost of transactions, they were able to take charge. Businesses could no longer drive the standard bill of fare. Blogs, social engineering, and networking were among a multitude of applets and widgets delivered to our touch-screen fingertips, causing us to lean toward the "me economy." The Internet-savvy consumer allows thrifty purse-conscious brands to cheaply emerge among titans that spent millions using expensive, traditional media to build their brands over the years. The Internet tossed many unprepared business leaders under the bus, while it allowed motivated and digitally savvy leaders to step on the gas and profit big-time. The hyper-accelerating global "me economy" thrives through consumer cloud platforms designed for highly profitable buying and selling, and the near instant promulgation of ideas, socialization, and personal monetization.

We are now traveling through the "ADD economy" (Attention-Deficit-Disorder economy), and will for years to come. Forgive me if you or anyone in your family or circle of friends has this terrible affliction, but the metaphor seems right to me. Consumers globally are perpetually either on a Blackberry, or a smart phone, or a PC, or a tablet, or a digital textbook, or on all of these while watching TV and answering an e-mail or telephone simultaneously. People managing all these devices and running their daily business and personal lives clearly disrupt a business's ability to sell, market, or lead a market. In the ADD economy, consumers as well as business leaders are all a mile wide in their attention span; only a few business immortals—Green Reign leaders—are at least an inch deep. Gaining mind share, brand share, and pocketbook share is becoming increasingly more difficult, especially as so many companies continue to lose ground through reliance on conventional advertising venues.

Business leadership with digital tools and expertise; new technologies and software; and new methods of stimulating sales, commanding a brand and market, and leading a team must navigate this new economy. Not just middle management but leadership must harness a multitude of information-retrieval techniques. Unless you, as the leader, understand and can command the capabilities of your human capital as well as your digital capital assets, you will crumble under the weight of your competitive disadvantage.

I've watched colleagues literally losing their minds, getting the shakes when they are sequestered in a business team getaway for a couple of days without their shiny digital tools. Remember, in this economy all web squatters, business pedestrians, and consumers have three lives: a home life, a business life, and a mobile life all wrapped around glowing digital technologies in various forms and sizes. Twenty-four hours a day we are all connected with these Internet-ready devices. It is hard to keep attention on discipline, details, and leadership. These magical mystery tools should firm the muscle of our resolve and ensure our competitive strength, motivating our teams to be faster, more agile, more effective, and more leadership-focused. For the digitally initiated and trained, the subject matter experts, it does just that; however, for those leaders sitting on the park bench drinking someone else's coffee, or casually embracing and studying digital tools, assets, and best practices to deploy for advantage, they do damage, not good. Green Reign leaders know they have an obligation to invest their personal time to focus their strategy and planning capabilities for their entire company.

For me, the ADD economy is highly relevant, but it also summons up memories of a song that The Guess Who wrote many years ago: "I got, got, got, got no time. " Many business leaders today are simply devastated, stuck in the stress-maelstrom of a deficient time cycle. It's not their fault, but it's truly their opportunity. It is a whirling cycle they cannot reveal in their reports or mention to their subordinates. It is a quiet, hidden problem that will be solved "if only I can find some spare time to build my knowledge muscle." While leaders yearn for quiet digital learning, and seek more time to understand the hundreds of new business-oriented digital technologies deployed by competitive camps almost instantaneously, more advanced digital tools dance and sing across competitors' fingers. For many, they're always too late, have good intentions, and suffer from a digital divide—a digital chasm.

It is just as inspiring to consider the change in consumer sentiment and the personal consumption (or lack of consumption) of advertising. Consumers, with very little time available between flipping channels and communicating on a variety of always-on devices, spend their time searching, watching, creating, buying, and socializing. Today, we skip advertisements—tripped right back into the cloud they came from—unless Green Reign Leadership delivers highly relevant and engaging messaging with perfect timing, offering value and emotional certitude. In essence, it takes a whole new level of engagement to attract consumer preference and determination to buy you, not them, in the ADD economy.

So, it is easy to say, "Let's dare to sell and dare to lead together, team." It is difficult to say this when all rules of the old business order have been either dismissed, confused, or eclipsed by a new land of digital tools. This demands a new energy for smarter, focused, and trained leadership, in a new land where consumer fingertips are in charge, not your advertising dollars. Consumers have paltry patience, constant digital connection, and little time to accept your ad, understand your brand, or choose your product rather than your competitors' offerings. This new land of instant-plenty allows consumer engagement globally, in a second. Green Reign Leadership is calibrated to address leaders, whether you are already heralded as apex competitors, whether you or team members are dancing on a competitive head of a pin, or whether you are hunting for the answer to get back the time you need to recover your digital mind and corresponding tool sets. Green Reign Leadership, when navigated properly, will always lead your team to a winning strategy. Excellence in Green Reign Leadership deliverables will lead to brilliant results in ensuing competitive advantage.

9

GREEN REIGN LEADERSHIP LESSONS

Women are like teabags. We don't know our true strength until we are in hot water!

Eleanor Roosevelt (1882–1962)

Just how do we leverage an advantage in our business future? How do we eliminate competitors? How do we tilt the digital divide in our favor? How do we ensure our reservoir of knowledge is correct? How do we galvanize our teams to take advantage of our window of opportunity? How do we put Green Reign Leadership into play to ensure a competitive advantage?

Leaders must be seen and must compete as Spartans. It is important to recognize and articulate leadership focus, intent, and the ability to foresee the future together as one team. The following Green Reign Leadership principles do not predict the future of your leadership, but instead lay out a proven roadmap designed to enhance and achieve greater rhythm and tempo toward achieving positive results and competitive advantage. These principles warm up the cold steel of the P&L statement;

open the door of achievable hope; and drive an entire organization to expand, grow, and profit together.

Let's start with building our core leadership foundation, to ensure we can dare to sell and lead for market advantage. The lessons ahead allow us to realize our greatest strengths as a team, as a competitive business nation. Green Reign Leadership's competitive foundation is designed to power-up sales, advertising and marketing return on investment (ROI), and all facets of management operations. Our principles are designed to lead in tough markets, through brave and sometimes unchartered opportunities, through mature competitors ready, willing and able to assault and battle hard your company effects, your company investment efforts.

Legs of Steel: What does it take to build shelf-space advantages in any marketplace? What does it take to ensure accelerating competitive advantages designed to exceed company goals?

The four-legged stool illustrates the Green Reign Leadership answer:

The first leg: finest quality, highly relevant consumer demanded products and services. The second leg: fluid, rational, profitable, and time-sensitive sales distribution channels. The third leg: unified, ambient push-and-pull marketing strategies. The fourth leg: is organizational leadership uniting a disciplined teams demanding to win, together. These business *legs of steel* must be consolidated into a single working unit, in which all are of equal value, operating at the same speed, functioning together as one integrated competitive force.

Make no mistake: this is a potent formula that is destined to fail if the wrong leadership orchestrates it. If just one of these legs of steel is misaligned or unequal in relation to the language, speed, and performance of the others, you will lose market opportunity. Demand will go silent as a graveyard, and the product and brand will be deemed a failure, based on "poor consumer demand."

Not so fast! The product failed because the stool was not steady, the legs were not steel, and the seat was not balanced. The problem was not necessarily the product or the consumer, but the sales strategy or something more.

Of course, these four steel legs have a seat: that seat represents your brand and, over time, your brand value. Only when you are outperforming your business and profit forecasts and gaining on your competitor's market share can you claim raising brand value, and claim that the seat of the stool is a true catalyst accelerating competitive market demand.

Accelerating success exemplifies a brand strengthening the value of the product. In most cases it is the product that builds and shapes the value of the brand. Brand identification over-values and strengthens any company's products. Its brand strength also allows the product to command a few more pennies than direct competitors. That's a very good position to be in—and also a very dangerous position to be in. Green Reign Leadership believes product strength and it's expected corresponding value proposition should always lead the brand. It's not long term profitable when a brand is managed and or forced to over-work and over-heat its efforts to try and lead a product's market validation, market opportunity. In many cases, if both the brand and product have equal vitality and strength, they can together achieve market share leadership. However, the majority of highly successful global market leaders build their business ventures on the backs of better, smarter, more differentiated and consumer valued products and price points. In best of breed, socially automatic mode, brands are strengthened and amplified based upon product preference, superiority, or differentiation (think Samsung, Coca-Cola, Apple, Starbucks, etc.). Green Reign Leadership believes it is axiomatic, that the promise of featured and juxtaposed product creation and values must be designed and tuned towards amplifying and muscling up brand value, ensuing brand infatuation.

The next chapter offers easy-to-understand-and-apply Green Reign Leadership principles. These principles are the rules of steel surrounding Green Rein sales, marketing, and operational leadership for products and services. They're used to ensure bedrock success, a competitive advantage within any business environment or sector, and the daily delivery and profitability of the freshest and most demanded products on the shelf. Each of these principles can stand alone as leadership clips or frames, or be galvanized with other complementary lessons relevant to your needs. Importantly, the ability to provide team members with highly relevant competitive wisdom will lead to competitive advantage. I will deliver all this information in short, relevant, and engaging data points.

10

TEN GREEN REIGN LEADERSHIP PRINCIPLES

Do not wait for leaders; do it alone, person to person.

Mother Teresa (1910–1997)

Consistent principles shape and support the overall business mission and guide urbane and effective leadership. Green Reign Leadership believes the following guiding principles will deliver the most effective short- and long-term team success. In addition, these leadership principles will deliver the clarity, purpose, and team fortitude necessary to achieve the business possible across the desktop, the workgroup, and the entire enterprise.

In its simplest definition, leadership is the formal action of leading a group of people or an organization to achieve a specified goal. And importantly, leaders may or may not have formal authority, but certainly possess charismatic influence based on their ability to interact, evoke action, shape behavior, share a vision, and create value. To be successful, you must convince your potential followers, not yourself or your superiors, that you are surely worthy of being followed, of being the ultimate leader.

The most significant, interpolative characteristics of superior Green Reign Leadership for comparison and consideration include the following personal traits. Green Reign Leaders are:

- **Knowledgeable**
- **Intelligent**
- **Flexible**
- **Compassionate**
- **Subject matter experts**
- **Intently focused**
- **High valued**
- **Trusted**
- **Inspirational**
- **Communicative**
- **Passionate**
- **Positive learners, caring teachers**
- **Customer centric**
- **Team centric**
- **Disciplined**
- **Caring and sharing with their team**
- **Driven**
- **Able to unleash capacity**

Specifically, ten effective principles and characteristics of Green Reign Leadership are:

1. **Leaders at every level** of organizations have the responsibility to *evaluate opportunity,* respect and take seriously competitors' business threats, ensure dedicated organizational leadership, and deploy best practices to unleash positive capacity and change that will result in positive fiduciary results. Essential to this vigorous leadership is the ability to clearly and precisely communicate your strategy and

expectations to all team members and business stakeholders. With the opportunity for success comes the danger of good intentions, which may ultimately fail. Our principles demand team credit for our successes; they also demand personal ownership for our losses. Don't blame; instead, accept the responsibility while consistently reevaluating your forecasts.

2. **It is critically important** to *listen, reflect, encourage, and accept feedback from team members* who have the means to amplify and protect your leadership strategy and stated business goals. There is both emotional and business capital flowing through the organizations responsible for the successful execution of "the plan." Leadership should expect team members to attentively listen to ensure their own clear understanding of the business plan and their ability to contribute to ensure best results. Never fear, but always revere highly energized and successful team members. Point to their determination and herald their successes among the team; be prepared to accept their opinions along the way to strengthen your overall competitive advantage.

3. **A leadership plan** offers no business value unless it is tied to *a completion date* with specific metrics such as enhanced operational benefits, increased speed, enhanced productivity, or expected financial results. Time is a leader's business heartbeat and crisp measurement of expectations and results. Stay on time and ensure all your team members are on time, all the time, to ensure the team delivers expected results.

4. **Leadership effectiveness** *must be companywide* and deployed with respect to enhance opportunities from the desktop to the department to the division and throughout the entire enterprise. It is important to keep a keen, disciplined eye on enterprise growth resulting from local desktop and departmental growth. If you enhance the local desktop and those results do not improve the enterprise,

then the money, time, and human capital deployed will favor your competition, while failing your own company's larger growth goals.

5. **Lead, do not shame.** If you want to be the leader, act like the leader twenty-four hours a day. Leadership, especially personal leadership, demands a highly balanced docent mentality, time-centered patience, and canny team navigation. It avoids department-wide criticism and discouragement. Always protect and energize the greater team, always discipline and disrupt the weak in a private one-on-one setting. Weak leaders without patience, knowledge, and vision utilize FUD (fear, uncertainty, and doubt) to de-motivate, correct the course of good-hearted efforts, and de-stimulate an entire team. In many ways, they punish intended productivity. Leadership's power and effectiveness is diminished when the FUD umbrella taints management tools. Poor leadership embarrasses and shames various members on the team again and again, causing "Mutiny on the Bounty" angst even among the best, and a lack of real production as employees cower and hide. This umbrage-based style of leadership destroys the entire team over time. Lead and teach, never shame or scold.

6. **Knowledgeable leadership offers power.** Building a formidable leadership team must include a circle of learning across multiple departments and asset disciplines. To grow your team requires you to gain agreement to move inside the company and cross-functional boundaries so that their leadership eye and future decisions are based on learned experience not learned guessing. *Grow your business strong by growing your team stronger.*

7. **Care about your team members and they will care about you. And care about your customers, make them part of your team and they too will care about you.** One of the three goals I have focused on and cared about for decades as a business leader is building a team of proud, stimulated leaders who are energized to come to work each day. I believe my caring, personal leadership focus mirrors the same focus

of each of my team members. Therefore together, we care about each other. We care about successful Green Reign Leadership together as one highly motivated team.

8. **First elaborate, then delegate.** As I will argue elsewhere in this book, "Clarity is sometimes a casualty." It amazes me when team members believe they understand a leader's command, but skew the vision just a few degrees off the expected mark. Leadership must take responsibility through accurate and decisive articulation and present clear expectations. Success begins and ends with the clarity of great leadership. In many cases, course corrections are forced by misinformation causing miscalculations, and further causing loss of competitive advantage.

9. **Show your quality in real time, all the time.** Leaders are responsible for *proving* their might: not pushing their might based on title, function, or responsibility, but on real teaching action. Correcting or grading team members is easy—the standard bill of fare. Proving there is a way to ensure success in a given responsibility based on action, though, is real Green Reign Leadership. I have often said to team members that they have a responsibility to push back on me when they have done all we have agreed to, yet still are not reaching or enjoying expected success. It is leadership's responsibility to help them and to teach them in good times and bad. It is my responsibility to ensure that they are personally successful, because I cannot be successful or achieve my business goals if my team members are failing. It is my obligation to also shepherd their determination, measurements, career paths, and ultimate success.

10. **Teach leadership principles early and often.** These important commandments set the stage for your team to pursue superior results on an individual level. This business constitution also builds muscle and long-term depth across your entire team. Leadership practices and deliverables constitute a twenty-four-hour-a-day commitment, especially in our newly charged, socially engineered business and personal worlds. All eyes and ears must be alert, because all

opportunities are always up for competitive grabs. Teach, because future teachers, future leaders need a deep, disciplined understanding and motivation to ensure their personal success, their entire team's advantage.

One of the greatest leadership honors in life is the opportunity to run with the Olympic torch. Peter Weedfald was honored to run and carry the Olympic torch flame through the streets of Florence Italy.

11

TEN RULES TOO SCOTCH YOUR COMPETITION

Live as if you were to die tomorrow. Learn as if you were to live forever.

Mahatma Gandhi (1869–1948)

There was a moment in time, many moons ago when I was a young, uninformed yet relentless salesman chasing opportunity through my rocky, wobbly, sloppy and competitively dampened legs. With personal strength in heart, mind and determination I pushed and pulled hard to build my sales capabilities but consistently found myself caught between the painful book ends of stress and humiliation enveloped by the miserable grotto of rejection and failure. Through this personal pain, unlike so many, I was so very fortunate to benefit from afflatus leadership determined to invest in me, to train me, to honor my efforts, to course correct my errors, to trust my personal demand to learn, to earn to compete, to deflect defeat. Leadership that cared about me personally cared about ensuring together we would be successful, together we would be valuable over time, together we would become a competitive sales force to reckon with. If not for this caring and sharing leadership, I would have been lost.

Like you, I am an ardent fan in building team muscle and competitive accord. Understanding and respecting each member's strengths and weaknesses to pinpoint needed support and a helping hand is at the core of building leadership momentum. Whether you define momentum in the language of market share, revenue, profit, brand value or otherwise does not matter. What matters most in leadership is to give back all that has been invested in you, to develop and docent new minds and hearts, to prevent future falls, to never allow another young mind to fall prey at the hands of the devil we call failure, demising of yet another hungry young business spirit.

The most successful leaders I know and have benefitted from believe in daring, caring and sharing their way towards delivering successful engagements. They believe in the greater spirit of generosity, in giving and teaching under the wide and elongated ribs of their experienced leadership umbrella. They respect and cherish their team, their brand and their customers. They even respect and study their direct competitors. But make no mistake, their positive investment in their team is truly designed to scotch and supplicate these same competitors, to gain market momentum. Green Reign Leadership believes you should respect thy competitor even while attacking their market positions, their market disciplines and their market advantage.

Having said this we serve up ten business rules designed to build and gain team advantage through smart building, sharing and teaching leadership disciplines:

1. **Conscript your heroes.** Hire only the finest performers at every level of your organization to ensure you have people with the necessary unbridled excitement, experience

and bandwidth to lead. In turn, you will be righteously challenged to lead, expected to lead, or you will be quite properly pushed out of the way by the positive spinning opportunities generated by these super-achieving heroes. We engage in a business world in which we pay for talented people because they are worth it. Remember, if you hire a non-hero, he or she will also hire non-heroes, building a team over time that will ultimately fail. You and I will never be able to do accomplish our goals in business without having an immensely talented group of allies, aides and team members within our company who have various talents we do not possess.

2. **Sales leadership in just seven-and-a-half minutes.** What is the perfect thread of reasoning and communication in the perfect sales presentation? What are the exact steps to achieve the perfect sales presentation? I title a presentation a "sales" presentation because the purpose of any presentation is to inform and sell the audience on your proposal, view for action, or results. This is an important point: please refrain from using the word "pitch" as a substitute for the word "presentation." When you say, "I want to pitch you on an idea," you immediately let down your guard, allowing your audience to see and expect what is coming. The defensive walls immediate go up; the audience knows you are going to try to be victorious over them. Your listeners hear the word "pitch" as a low-class salesman's approach to a serious subject, as opposed to a Green Reign leader offering options and opportunities.

The seven easy and perfect leadership steps below answer the core questions above regarding a sales presentation. Each step of the selling presentation process builds effectively and formidably on the keen observations of opportunity, with a corresponding proposal based on real-time research observations for opportunity and positive growth:

Open–Market–Buyers–Competition–Summary–Proposal–Close

What's scary is how little time you have to achieve your objective in any sales call. Your *open* must be creative, focused, and highly relevant to audience's world order, not yours. You must discuss *market* conditions, dynamics, and changes that may reshape opportunity positively or negatively. The subject and profile of the *buyers'* community is critical: Who are they? What do they want? What are their expectations? Where do they shop? How much will they spend? Why would they buy your lettuce and not someone else's? Remember, it's okay to reveal *competition* advantage or disadvantage as part of the good-faith aspect of your presentation. The *summary* allows you to take the pulse of your audience and seek agreement to your market, buyers, and competitive points. It also allows you to accomplish a minor point, closing with your prospect on relevant points of discussion, moving them from prospects to long-term successful and profitable customers.

At this point, you need to *propose* the purchase, or sales upgrade, with a very thorough and relevant proposal, better known as a "talking paper." It is a talking paper because you never hand the proposal to a prospect and ask him or her to read it, you walk the person through every line item, talking through the proposal's features and benefits so you may best command the next and most important step; the *close* of the sale. Most importantly, you must always remember that you must *earn* the right to ask for the order, to close the audience on your proposal.

If you have not earned the right through relevancy, in steps one through six, you will surely fail when you try to *close* the order—your proposal. If you have earned the right, you need to ask for the order directly and firmly. It sounds something like this: "Well Bob, according to this research report I shared earlier, more people are health conscious and are turning to lettuce as the center of their dietary requirements *(open section)*. Based on the increasing market demand for certain types of lettuce that I presented today, there certainly should be an opportunity for us to offer yet another variety of lettuce for your shelves, one designed to complement our current line of vegetables and distinguish ourselves from our direct competitors *(market section)*. We do know from tracking our other retail customers that this new and fresh lettuce product line is in high consumer demand and in addition, is highly profitable *(buyer section)*. The best news, Bob, is your two main competitors are not carrying our new line, creating a further reason for health-conscious shoppers to drive to your store to ensure they will have an opportunity to purchase the freshest lettuce on the shelf *(competition section)*."

"So, as we agree, you are seeking a more competitive lettuce for your shelves, which will drive more buyers to your store seeking the freshest lettuce, which they cannot find on your competitors' shelves *(summary section)*. Based on your demand for the freshest lettuce on the shelf to drive more consumers to your store, I propose an initial order of X with a special kick-off profit initiative of Y to be delivered on Z date to kick-start your competitive program *(proposal section)*. May I place this order for you? *(close section)*."

Selling and marketing the freshest lettuce on the shelf is like painting a room. Once all the preparation of spackling *(open)*, scraping *(market)*, sanding and taping *(buyers)*, is complete, painting the room—make that asking for the order—is very straightforward and easy to complete. You will find by holding to these firm steel features of Green Reign Leadership discipline that at first it will take you one hour to earn the right for the order. Over time, with practice, you will become a master of the same sale, in only seven-and-a-half minutes. Highly successful financial companies who spend years building an incredible financial services business on the pillars of great selling, marketing, and customer service understand the power of seven-and-a-half minutes to close the sale. They understand that we are all salespeople every day of our lives. We are selling our ideas, plans, and enthusiasm to those whom we come in contact with. The sales presentation's relevance and good-faith information ensures a presenter's right to ask for the order. Based on the success of so many financial institutions, these seven steps, designed to *earn the right* to ask for the sales order, works very effectively. But what about selling through objections during our own business presentations?

In business, an objection is a request for more information: If you object to something I ask of you, it's not your fault, it's my fault. An objection is simply a request for more information. It is a request for clarity and a deeper level of understanding during an exchange or negotiation. Many salespeople surrender to "failure" when attempting to articulate goods or services, then find they are walled off into a defensive position. Remember, clarity is sometimes a casualty of promotion, especially if you are unable to handle the objection. Turn objections to your advantage through these three steps: clarify the objection, restate the objection, and finally ask a highly relevant question regarding the objection. Take personal control: navigate objections to create successful engagements and to create heightened value. Remember, it takes practice. It takes great motivation and hard work to address and overcome objections. Vince Lombardi understood this. He often remarked of the importance to stand and cheer for the doer, the achiever—the one who recognizes the challenge and does something about it. A true achiever recognizes the challenge of an objection and is well prepared to overcome it with more relevant and enticing information.

3. **Brand is the refuge of the ignorant.** Can a photograph of an overweight man sell you a digital camera? Or will the overweight man representing your product and brand confuse and disrupt your demand cycle as the consumer's mind starts wondering about his or her own weight and thinking about whether it's time to diet? As your potential customer stares at the man's belly, your brand and product become nothing more than background noise. Too many companies seem to think metaphors in advertising drive competitive advantage. Think again. Since *brand is truly the refuge of the ignorant*, ensure you design every aspect of your brand and product advertising to focus on your greatest hero: your product and services. Otherwise stronger more recognized brands-logos will be automatically advantaged

even against your better product and better price. Don't focus on exposing or selling the hanging rump roast of your overweight model. **The simple formula for failure:** go esoteric with your advertising and disrespect your product and brand value by ignoring them. We call this road to failure: "logo lazy." **The simple formula for success:** present your product, offering, its competitive product and price advantages clearly and dearly to drive both sales and brand value. If you go the logo lazy way, just watch your demand run away, rump roast and all, gone faster than you can imagine to a very special and secure warehouse that we in the industry call "the warehouse of distressed inventory."

Consider one of the world's greatest animators, Walt Disney, a man whose forty years of service to brands such as Mickey, Donald, Goofy, Bambi and so many other wonderful characters, won Disney Studios forty-eight Academy Awards. Would he or did he ever advertise with an overweight man to build the brand of Mickey Mouse? No, never. Walt was a brand and demand genius, as well as a great master creator of sweet dreams for children and grownups. He was also a wonderful brand builder. He gathered all his incredible character brands within the master-brand of his Magic Kingdom for all to enjoy, in a place where each character (brand) could become stronger each day by drawing upon the others. He ensured over time that no man, woman, or child would ever be ignorant of the mighty brand called Disney. Walt was known to say: "The more you are like yourself, the less you are like anyone else. This is what makes you unique." These are wise words to apply when building brands and accelerating demand. Remember, if you focus uniquely on your hero-products' features and benefits, then consumers will do the same. Otherwise, your most important buyer will surely be left ignorant of the value proposition of your brand, product, and services. In a fast-paced world, ignorance can leave you and your brand in the losing position in the pack. I'll bet the unique brand power of Mickey, Minnie, Goofy, and even Donald still make you stop and smile, and think: M-I-C-K-E-Y...M-O-U-S-E. Simply brilliant!

4. **Complexity is the refuge of the unsure.** You know these leaders. You have worked for them. They don't know the subject matter in depth—in marketing, sales, finance—and they don't know the appropriate course of action. They tend to make simple decisions complex.

Complexity in leadership can be recognized and best resolved through relevant education. As Malcolm S. Forbes said, "Education's purpose is to replace an empty mind with an open one." Great leadership always has an open, learning mind, to ensure that complexity is replaced with simplicity and education is a two-way street: leadership to team members, team members to leadership. There is nothing complex about it. Malcolm's son Steve Forbes said, "The real source of wealth and capital in this new era is not material things—it is the human mind, the human spirit, the human imagination and our faith in the future." In business, sometimes *clarity is a casualty*. Without education, complexity will remain the refuge of the unsure, and clarity of purpose will give way to complexity that foils good intentions and ensures failed purposes. The sign over my desk for years has one word inscribed, a word that drives our team's competitive advantage: "Simplify." Get some simplicity and shed complexity today.

5. **Focus on your customers and they will focus on you.** Not much more to say other than if you treat your customers with excellence in support and care, your team and company shall be rewarded with more business, higher profitability.

6. **The Internet is Darwin on speed.** In the new information economy, knowledge and content are *commodities* that can be instantly transformed into both revenue and profit-generating *security*. The Internet becomes the new supply-chain distribution model for hyper-accelerated competitive advantage. Companies fall back on the promise of broad-based television advertising as a demand-building tool, despite the fact that the medium is outmoded and incredibly overpriced compared with the Internet. Don't miss the power of the Internet to push—and pull—customers

to you, nearly instantly. And the internet as a highly competitive and targeted medium offers broadcasting, narrow casting and micro casting advertising all at once. Go ahead and try that on television.

Some companies do not understand the bedrock business value to command the power from within, the tornado-like, highly competitive ability of the Internet to drive revenues, profitability, brand, and distribution. Think about this: companies may outsource their entire customer Internet-facing commerce engine, and infrastructure.

Amazon is an incredible model of excellence. Jeff Bezos built the e-model for all to appreciate and emulate—a model built on the foundation of consumer choice, speed of execution, service, and support. He shredded the rulebook for customer interaction through highly relevant automatic Internet commands of choice and value. He defined the Internet's hyper-speed, efficient business model all tied to best in class customer service.

Understand every facet of the internet and corresponding competitive tools. Company's and corresponding brands must first and foremost create, manage, command and control their internet destiny, daily. Own it, command it and integrate it through your sales, marketing and communications strategy disciplines. Whatever you do, don't lose or misplace this competitive power within your core company strategy.

7. **There is no difference between sales and marketing; they are the same.** They are 100 percent bimodal, with the nature of their core DNA rooted in the same five steps to ensure the fastest, most competitive, and most profitable success.

The five mirroring steps to ensure successful sales or advertising results are:

Attention—Interest—Conviction—Desire—Close

In essence, if you are granted *60 minutes* to present and sell your freshest lettuce face to face then your goal must surely be to gain your customer's attention, interest, conviction, and desire

followed by asking for the order, (the close). If you are successful through this selling (60 minutes) and or advertising (30 seconds) thread, meaning you gain the audience intense attention,
their keen interest, their personal conviction and their emotional
desire for your products or brand you are then able to ask for the
order. Go ahead; you earned it, close this sale.

In marketing, take note of highly successful advertising campaigns. In any advertisement, you have *thirty seconds* to get
your prospective buyer's attention, interest, conviction, desire,
and to close the sale on either your product or your brand, or
some form of direct action. If you fail to gain attention and or
interest in the first *10 seconds*, the viewer turns away, flips the
channel, or turns the page, and or simply ignores your message. This means your hard earned advertising budget has been
wasted.

In contrast yet complimentary to advertising, sales is granted
60 minutes for their customer presentation, not 30 seconds. And
again, you have *60 minutes* to get the prospective buying customers <u>attention, interest, conviction, desire, and to close</u> the
sale on either your product or your brand, or some form of direct
action. If you fail to gain their attention and or interest in the first
10 minutes, the prospect excuses himself stating "oh I forgot, I
have another meeting to attend: nice meeting you." This means
your hard earned time, travel expenses and sales budget have
been wasted.

Of course, reading these critical steps of the sales and process is step one in mastering them. But it takes an assiduous,
fanatical commitment to practice these steps to deliver a successful competitive advantage within seconds. Warren Buffet
posed a question that shows how to achieve long-term success.
"Are you a fanatic? A manager must care intensely about running
a first-class operation; if his golf game is what he thinks about
while shaving, the business will show it." Focus, practice, and
succeed in gaining competitive customer attention, interest, conviction and desire, ensuring the close. This is the way to succeed
in Green Reign Leadership.

8. **Leaders need boundless sensitivity and rugged constitutions.**
   To seed excellence the successful leader must be consistently sensitive to the needs of each team member through his or her daily performance. That includes awareness of emotional capital ups and downs, not just overall value to the team. To ensure a successful and lasting future, leaders must be sensitive to each team member's needs, understanding his or her personal as well as business dreams. A rugged leadership backbone balanced between passion and expected results ensures that appropriate course corrections are timely, expected, and successful. A rugged, highly disciplined, personal constitution is always needed and expected to ensure goals, budgets, individual commitments and strategies are on focus and are achieved.

9. **Expect to win and you surely will.** Winning is a full-time contact sport, that business leaders create and administer unequally and unfairly in the arena of competitive advantage. Superior leadership includes recognizing those who believe in their hearts they can win and who commit their lives to ensuring they do. Invest those individuals with your personal wisdom: it is well worth it. Over time you will create a stable of winners who expect to win. Remember, people remember you for how you end up, not all the years of your success. Expect to win each and every day. Instill and promote this mind set throughout your team and you surely will win, again and again. But remember, success in life has nothing to do with what you gain in life or accomplish for yourself. It's what you do for others." Expect to win through your leadership, your heart, and the hearts and minds of your team members. They will in turn expect to win, for you.

10. **Focus on leadership and leadership will focus on you.** There is a legacy of quicksilver business decisions that prove to be the foundation and underpinnings of fallen leadership. Quantum direction changes from the top are unreliable if they are not founded in consensus, sound business practice, and sound company confidence. Further, misanthropic

leadership will scorch your employee roster, destroying the young and brave new future of your business. Be clear, be concise, be intelligent, be bold, be relevant, be open, be passionate, be careful, but mostly, be *trustworthy*. This is the bedrock foundation of leadership. Joe Torre, manager of the most winning baseball team in the world, the New York Yankees, says: "Communication is the key to trust and trust is the key to teamwork in any group endeavor, be it in sports, business, or family." He's right. When the leader focuses and delivers true leadership, the entire team will lead the competition. After all, the Yankees won four World Series' victories under Joe's leadership.

Peter Weedfald honored to stand and promote with Yankees Coach Joe Torre and Mayor Rudy Giuliani during a fund raising evening in New York City benefitting The Joe Torre Safe At Home Foundation and Saint Vincent's Hospital.

12

WHO ARE YOU?

Great trials seem to be a necessary preparation for great duties.

James Thomson (1802–1884)

It would not be hard to metaphorically define business strategy as the varying orchestrations and melodic personalities of musicians from years past or today. To succeed in music, within any style, there always needs to be a unique product (music) proposition…or maybe not.

Perhaps when Pete Townshend and Roger Daltrey of The Who first united musical forces back in 1964, they were not worried about or planning *uniqueness*; perhaps they were simply energized by their *single driving force* and determination in the language of *expression*. Perhaps much-heralded musical superstars gain preference through a duopoly of uniqueness and expression—not by planning this union, but rather as a result created by audience demand, dreams, and preference passionately and warmly translated into product sales.

Well, what about those of us not in the music business? What about those of us who must face the daily cold steel of the P&L, hunting for success, pining for opportunity, balancing between competitors' unique products, expressive advertising, and the daily scorching price-point pressure? Hey, what about us?

In any business with any product or service offering, we know the driving force to ensure success can be summed up in one word: *focus*. Focus defines the mission; focus expresses and matures the profitable boundaries; focus ensures market relevancy; focus mitigates competitive muscle. Focus is, in itself, strategy.

Since most of us are not rock 'n' roll, hip-hop, or global-music artists (although it is always nice to dream), we remain business focused on ten far-reaching steps to ensure formidable market and profit advantage. *To best remember the ten Green Reign rules for market advantage, I've added memory hooks from the prophetic words of The Who to best stimulate and articulate ten more Green Reign Leadership principles:*

Pete Townshend, Peter Weedfald, Roger Daltrey, FrancesAnn and Tara Weedfald celebrate the musical magic and united giving generosity of The Who.

1. Focus on a specific product offering: no *"Fiddling About!"* Don't be a mile wide; be a profitable and highly focused inch deep.
2. Address and serve a defined market opportunity. Be open to new, complementary products that are needed or demanded, and connect with the *"Magic Bus"* of your core focus.
3. Make every sales and marketing touch point deliver your competitive features, advantages, and benefits. Focus on your product as your market hero; focus on your brand as your product's emotional capital. This way no one will ever ask: *"Who Are You?"*
4. Clarity is sometimes a casualty. Define who you are, where and how you are focused, and the core mission at hand, so that all team members, as well as your profit and loss statement, *"Won't Get Fooled Again!"*
5. Relevant market, product, and consumer research augur competitive opportunity and allows any leader to profess: *"I Can See for Miles and Miles!"*
6. *"I'm free!"* Be media and editorial driven. Take advantage of all *free* digital, social, and relevant global medium resources to promote and fuel your products.
7. Manufacturing, production, and supply chain expertise is any organization's greatest strength. All is possible as long as the mission exploits and justifies production capabilities. *"You Better You Bet"* establish advantage through manufacturing excellence by betting on your production leadership's competitive advantage.
8. Channel your focus and energy on the right distribution. A rational channel strategy offers competitive expansion, profit protection, and long-term market share dominance. You can't be a market *"Pinball Wizard"* if you can't control the ball.
9. To be a *"Happy Jack,"* focus on market data to best forecast, pursue, navigate, invest, and align with your best, most profitable opportunities.

10. *Hire your heroes* to ensure your results. Spartan employees are full of energy, focus, determination, and passion to rock. Recognize you cannot simply and easily *"Substitute"* their talents and contributions.

Well, that was fun and a rock and roll guerdon for me personally, to incorporate the incredible emotional capital of The Who into the intense sobriety of our business lives. Now it's time to celebrate and express our own uniqueness and business leadership; all together now: *"Long Live Rock!"*

13

TEN PROFITABLE PRINCIPLES

A good head and good heart are always a formidable combination.

Nelson Mandela (1918-)

Principles of Profitable Green Reign Leadership

S uccessful, profitable leaders are first and foremost, technically proficient and market relevant. They are characteristically and continually strengthening their personal leadership assets while always taking responsibility for their business actions. Profitable leaders make very sound and timely decisions and set the example as "can do, will do, done" company role models. They communicate kinetically, train consistently and ensure an open book policy of the business forecast, the annual budget, and expected goals in measured metrics.

The most successful, effective, and profitable leaders share results, good or bad through a monthly team review. The valued leader is in constant launch mode, corrective mode, and truth mode as he or she informs both positive and negative feedback to his or her team to ensure that they attain the most profitable results. Green Reign Leadership's ten principles to ensure profitable business results are:

1. **Rhythm impact.** Tempo creates business advantage and business winners. Tempo also creates business losers. Relentless focus on speedy and efficient supply chain management proves that time itself can be a bumbling rust agent or a mind-boggling accelerator for market supremacy. The creation of new stockholder value, designed to hyper-accelerate results, must be accomplished through highly balanced rhythm impact. Rhythm impact also allows greater focus toward creating and delivering new products and replacing old ones that may have lost their speed of competitive advantage, or which may no longer be fresh.

Rhythm impact is not a solitary art form designed just for tallying inventory turns. Rhythm impact must be deployed as a multimodal business weapon, speedily mirroring all areas to ensure the freshest lettuce will always be on the shelf, daily—the freshest product, fastest distribution, and even faster advertising and marketing in tempo with product and distribution. Rhythm impact illustrates hyper-change and hyper-growth. Rhythm impact aggregates business strengths and opportunities, creating the fast-paced art of the possible: the freshest lettuce on the shelf, every day. William Shakespeare said in "Macbeth," "If you can look into the seeds and say which grain will grow and which will not, speak to me then." It's time to shred the old schoolbook discussion of supply chain management and deploy the business power of rhythm impact.

2. **Increases in productivity deliver increases in profitability.** Fiduciary responsibility typically shreds human capital as

the textbook correction most often used to promote the bottom line. In reality, Board of Directors members should be paragons of virtue, ejecting the CEO whose leadership is failing, rather than decreasing employee headcount as the best method to stabilize and resurrect a sinking P&L. When a company finds itself in the profit-recession business, blame and reconciliation must be at the top of the business, not at the bottom.

Profits provide an early warning system that becomes transparent when the sales organization over steers toward earth-scorched pricing for your newest, most competitive freshest lettuce. This low-scale pricing, expected to increase profitable inventory turns, instead leaves limp, stale lettuce in your warehouse. In accountants' eyes, decreasing your headcount will, "increase the productivity" of remaining employees, who must suddenly add ex-employee functions to their daily routines. It will not, however, solve the more important issue of accelerating long-term consumer demand, where profits and real productivity gains unite to form the covenant of market demand with market-making opportunity. "Things do not happen; things are made to happen," said President John F. Kennedy. Increasing productivity with greater education, focus on best practices, and concentration on competitive opportunities will yield greater profitability. Profit will only happen if you focus on highly productive engagements.

3. **Strategy is the mettle you must shine every day.** Strategy is the loneliest discipline of business leadership. Many times fear of rejection from the top prevents implementing team strategy and direction. There is also valid fear that the cold eye and fast pace of business may frustrate or fracture the foundation of a corporate vision, leading to uncertainty, doubt, confusion, and even beleaguered employees. A corporation's precise strategic direction should be viewed as the most important reservoir of shared knowledge and the most important leadership mettle for all employees.

Ensuring all employees are informed and in focused agreement with said strategy will allow the entire team to produce and shine the medal together.

Remember; never be satisfied with how things are this day, this week, this month or even this quarter. The only way to ensure sluggish and rust prone complacency doesn't have a seat at the table in your business life is to polish the medal of your strategy, your goals, your brand, and your team members with aggressive expectations, daily.

4. **The fire in the belly.** True champions have a cluster of high-spirited ambitions and intentions deep in their hearts and minds. This internal infrastructure of power, alight at all hours of the day and night, is a special gift that cannot be bought, rented, faked, and purchased. The most fortunate champions, with serendipity sprinkled generously through their genes, benefit from both the mental and physical power of this brightly burning flame. You can observe their speed during practice. You can admire their keen intellect in their balanced, yet competitively advantaged decisions. You may be amazed by their superior performance versus other titans who are competing to win. You can easily recognize this amazing power, the fire in the belly. Wake up each morning and look in the mirror to see if you, too, have this important flame burning brightly in your heart, mind, and belly. There are certainly many ways to articulate this blazing advantage. This fire in the belly for leadership works and accents best when you are able to energize those whom you lead. Build your business and your leadership arsenal through the fire in the belly: try to get some.

5. **Respect apex predators, even if they do not respect you.** The most dangerous detour in business occurs when management sniffs over, rejects, or ignores competitors who may break through the proverbial market share wall. Those competitors, in most cases, use expensive borrowed

interest in the form of consultants and new hires focused on exposing your weakest points and finding your company's crack in the wall. Great competitors are quietly in knowledgeable conflict, yet highly respectful of each other. Be careful. The most aggressive and focused apex predators may seem to ignore your company even as they vacuum out your business in a multitude of aggressive ways. To protect against such apex predators, build your own wall of sales, marketing, and operational advantages focused on building your business, not on tearing down your competitors. And most importantly, learn from your competitors, from their competitive advantage, from just what they are doing so right, free of charge. Be focused on both their strengths and weaknesses and demand and train your team to do the same. Remember, everyone is doing something right it's your role as the leader to do it even better. Respect apex predators, even if they do not respect you. Take their free, smart market lessons and turn them into opportunities, accelerated competitive advantage.

6. **Consistency is the refuge of the unsure.** The roadmap to change begins with a determination to suspect false ideologue viewpoints trembling with validation due to nervous and unsure intentions. Continuing a strategy or tactical course of action, including using the same team that built the former unsuccessful roadmap, is simply a prelude to failure in the majority of cases. Proper balance and orchestration in leadership includes the ability to recognize consistent programs that deliver exceptional value versus programs that consistently cause stagnation and reversals of fortune. Leadership without experience in varying subjects may see consistency as a business virtue. Consistency is the comforting refuge of the unsure, and will lead to loss of market share, your best employees when they seek dynamic leadership, and a future. A great man, Confucius, once said: "It is only the wisest and most stupid who cannot change." His point? The wise

man knows when to be consistent, but also has the will to change, while the dumb man remains consistent, hoping something will actually change for the better in absence of a plan.

7. **Emotional capital is very inexpensive fuel.** Leadership is sometimes presented as the ability to offer penetrating insights across a variety of departments, workgroups, and throughout an entire enterprise. Leadership is also viewed as the ability to deliver strategic commands with boundless sensitivity and a rugged constitution. With confident and effective decision-making tied to highly supportive infrastructure, leadership can accelerate and build valiant futures. However, leadership pollsters many times show an inability to define best practices in leadership in regards to emotional fidelity. Business writers have hardly even brought this vitally important area of leadership into consideration. Many leaders avoid building close relationships with their subordinates because they fear that they may have to reprimand or censure the same employee someday.

The leader's power to exert pressure within employee relationships based on poor performance should be viewed as an act of strength and courage. The lack of power to openly praise employees, to ignore pumping the visceral fuel of emotional capital for their exceptional performance, should be viewed as blindness to the obvious: many leaders fear their kindness will be mistaken for weakness. Green Reign Leadership believes in reviewing every good idea from every person in the organization and disallowing management styles that suppress and intimidate this important practice. In business and through leadership, emotional capital, the dignity of exchanged knowledge and the extension of team participation is very inexpensive business and highly potent business fuel.

8. **Complexity is the refuge of the unsure.** Conventional leadership wisdom should support clear and concise strategy with fidelity threaded through the entire organization.

Every key staff member should be able to deliver the central strategy in one concise sentence, in one minute, within five scripted minutes, and even within one slide-elaborated presentation over the course of an hour. As intrepid as this may sound, a common reason for the failure to communicate such an important element of the business is a pervasive leadership virus known as *complexity*.

If leadership is incapable of reaching a consensus and promoting a concise, relevant core strategy, then a propensity for complex misdirection will prevail throughout the organization. Indeed, the unsure will find refuge in a complex and jumbled strategy—the source of doomed results. Many times top leadership falls flat, falls failure because they were so focused on the next position opportunity that they didn't get the current job done. Management should view and experience personal performance as a measure of potential, not potential as a measure of performance. Sometimes business complexity is pervasive because a company lacks personal leadership focus, not just because it lacks leadership communications. Complexity is truly the refuge of those who are unsure about their next position and their ability to communicate directly, simply.

9. **The best opportunities lie in danger.** New opportunities lead to increased demand, but real new opportunities are not for the faint of heart. If you don't have mature leadership coupled with a bedrock foundation in a particular subject, you'll never be opportunistic. If the very best opportunities did not lie in dangerous territory, then everyone would be successful. Calculating, measuring, and planning levels of risk is as important as calculating, measuring, and planning levels of opportunity.

10. **There is a difference between a condition and an objection.** It amazes me that, in so many circumstances, senior leadership and its team members treat a business *condition* the same way they treat a business *objection*. An objection based on a request is simply "a request for more

information." If a client tells you "no" or objects to your proposal, you have an obligation to deliver the relevant missing information to allow your audience to make an informed decision. You can and should overcome objections. Objections are truly an informed leader's best proxy to ensure victory, designed as a quid quo pro victory for both seller and buyer, for both employer and employee.

You usually cannot overcome a condition so easily. You cannot change, augment or clear a condition through simple gestures, suggestions, or clarifications. A condition can be very restricting, limiting, or a modifying circumstance that causes a major stipulation in agreement, causing a change to a stated event or expected covenant. A condition provides a map of the terrain you must work through and within; a description of the details that you (or your customer) can't or are unable to change.

Therefore, in business, be flexible in command to win each and every *objection* tossed your way. However, respect and manage all *conditions* as potential granite walls with no keys to open the doors of opportunity, and no keys to turn conditions into successes.

14

TECHNOLOGY DISRUPTION PORTENDS OPPORTUNITY

Nearly all men can stand adversity, but if you want to test a man's character, give him power.

Abraham Lincoln (1809—1865)

There are many galaxy-class superstars who led us through interplanetary adventures on the small and big screens, through imaginary visions of very cool technologies yet to come. We are all truly tech heads seeking and enjoying technology hyper-speeds and feeds in the language of instant communications, content, social karma, and beam me up instantly dreams of transport. We all enjoy trying and buying the latest advanced technology and electronics products in retail stores and online. We are right to seek new, fresh, cool and advanced products to exercise our dreams, feed our passion for speed, color, content, the next frontier. If this is your way to hip hop across galaxies on various size screens, be aware, you are not alone.

Since the imaginative days of what might be as depicted across movie screens, a multitude of software and hardware technologies have changed the brand and product opportunities landscape within the consumer electronics product category. Our own technology savvy tech frontier is causing market disruption, accelerated market opportunity, causing P&L tensions and strategic risk throughout traditional retail environments. In fact, these futuristic hardware, software and cloud centric products are serious catalysts to fiduciary and SG&A (selling, general, and administrative expenses on any profit-and-loss statement) disruptions for retailers and manufacturers, on a global scale. Or, perhaps as Green Reign Leadership believes, these tech tools are the new weapon of opportunity choice for smart, growth minded business leaders.

Disruptive as well as opportunistic hardware products include smart phones, tablets, slates, and netbooks, along with newly connected Internet televisions streaming to and from mammoth back-end serving and storage cloud farms. Opportunistic software products include instant access content: applets, widgets, games, movies, music, and a vast array of cloud computing applications. And of course a multitude of trail's and way's to profitable commerce.

I recall we never thought about business risk and potential competitive opportunity while sleeping and dreaming about the so many awesome space voyages across television and movie screens. We never imagined that in our business, risk never sleeps and never tires and those who can command the once seemingly cool technology machines will fill the cash register with profitable engagements.

"So Mr. Spaceman, how has space age technology changed business America?"

1. We have entered a new consumer-centric *price transparency* world that benefits consumers. However, it causes grave disruption for any retailers still relying on old consumer traffic patterns, purchasing behaviors and consumption models.

2. *Past necessities are becoming obsolete.* Old consumer products such as camera film, paper, stamps, envelopes, magazines, newspapers, CDs, and DVDs are rapidly being replaced or augmented by smart phones, smart slates, tablets, and smart TVs, allowing consumers to instantly enjoy a multitude of home, mobile, and business activities through varying electronic devices.

3. Smart phones cause disruption. *The four walls of the retail store have become porous.* Last year, consumers simply dropped a $184.85 global positioning system into their retail shopping carts. Today, consumers take out their smart phone and point their cameras at the product UPC code. An onboard application recognizes it is viewing a UPC code, records it, and then provides both details and reviews about the product, the prices at websites, and the prices at stores nearby. Talk about disruptive–this is amazing. The exact item on another website is only $106.75, with no shipping charges, free gift wrapping and no state sales tax. Smartphone reckoning represents a revolution in retailing. The retailer's traffic and profit advantages versus internet alternatives are eroding because of new space age technologies.

4. Traditionally valued *consumer brands* are consolidating, and in some cases collapsing, disappearing, and declining across retail shelves. New products and unknown brands are creating, stimulating and articulating advanced forms of highly valuable brand recognition without the usage of conventional marketing wisdom. Social engineering, networking and calibration of new brands and products flash fast globally and can be experienced and purchased through thousands of cloud based internet commerce engines, instantly. Traditionally valued brands must fight for their brand and product strength and opportunities through these same socially charged locations to survive, to thrive.

5. A multitude of retailers are embracing private-label product agreements and strategies, allowing for complete

control of costs, pricing, line logic assortment, advertising, communications, and brand positioning to better compete. With historic brands having to work harder and faster every hour to remain viable to distinguish their greater value through the hyper-blur of a world with billions of internet messages a day, more profitable, less expensive to build private label brand opportunities are accelerating rapidly.

6. The retail sector was an economic highlight for 2010, posting its strongest performance since 2004 (according to The Bureau of Census, January 2011). Sales during the year rose 7.9 percent year over year (YOY), a pickup from the 5.1 percent gain during 2009 and the dismal 11.1 percent decline during 2008. However, the strongest gain on a percentage basis occurred in electronic shopping, which grew at a rate of 16.4 percent. The ongoing shift from brick-and-mortar stores to electronic shopping is supporting the longer-term growth strategy of more profitable non-store retail models.

7. The TV business is rapidly aggregating new profit pools through a variety of Internet content downloads. There is a dedicated turf war between cable and satellite content providers, TV manufacturers, retailers and internet content providers for the profitable delivery of content to consumers through connected TV's. Green Reign Leadership believes from empirical results, that there is more profit to gain in cloud based content downloads then in selling physical television, tablet or cell phone hardware products.

8. Traditional retailers with hefty SG&A costs are P&L challenged. Lower-priced, lower-margined products breaking into the market, greater online price and service competition, once hearty and essential retail store traffic moving to online "endless-aisle" shopping venues, and smart phones allowing instant price comparisons are causing retail disruption.

9. Single product category (just consumer electronics, just food, just clothing, just tires, etc.) retail business models

are traffic challenged. Consumer traffic is the heartbeat for any retailer. This spells competitive opportunity for multi-category retailers, both in physical stores and online.

10. *The connected TV mirrors the razor-blade business.* The next battleground for hearts, minds, and wallets of consumers will be through connected Internet TVs. Making a profit on downloading content through TV screens is now juicing profits on TVs. In essence, the TV business is becoming the razor-blade business. In the razor business you promote your razor grips to sell and profit from your blades. In this case, Internet content purchased represents the profitable "blade" business when downloaded onto TV screens. This is just one example of where the new profit frontier lives and thrives.

Green Reign Leadership believes our cloud based vista of opportunity is vast, wide and deep space however, very differently derived and articulated from years past. Our new twenty-four-hour-a-day world of instant information, entertainment, product pricing, product reviews, and personal connectivity is disruptively morphing the consumer electronics business as well as the traditional retail business. *Smart brands* will seek and find deeper, more meaningful consumer relationships through smart devices, supporting channel-buying preference. Profitable brands will capitalize through increasing productivity; delivering profitability increases best realized through the instant push and pull Internet thrusters.

Profit pools for manufacturers versus retailers certainly differ; however, they have traditionally run in concert and in noncompeting harmony. We are at the advent of manufacturers selling against retailers through their own stores and commerce clouds with stimulating product and price advantages. This creates a new highly dynamic and challenging level of channel conflict versus a time of more controlled and rational channel strategies. In all of this change, opportunity abounds. With the entrance of profitable widget and applet downloads, of cheap but useful applications, games, movies, and music, opportunity abounds and accelerates. Especially for the right brand, with the right product, with the right channel and pricing strategy, opportunity truly and expressly abounds.

Through the multitude of space adventures and travel we have experienced and enjoyed on the big screens for decades many other final-frontier friends were harbingers of our disruptive and consumer-beneficial destinies. They gave us a glimpse again and again of how our business lives would be disrupted, changed and challenged. Today, as promised in space stories, the Internet and a multitude of glowing smart boxes and screens are disrupting business models, while at the same time orchestrating new opportunity frontiers through a multitude of smart tools, turning successful leaders into pilots of the Internet storm.

15

DOES THE SONG REMAIN THE SAME?

I am so clever that sometimes I don't understand a single word of what I am saying.

Oscar Wilde (1854 – 1900)

In a business environment, revenue, profit, and market share begin and end with consumers. This means that *knowing, understanding, and applying consumer trends and insights will forever be the holy grail* for business and marketing professionals.

Robert Plant and Peter Weedfald meet in New York to discuss ways to help others through fund raising and giving opportunities. It was an incredible honor to meet with this worldwide musical genius and melodic leader.

Led Zeppelin, an English rock band formed in 1968, consisted of guitarist Jimmy Page, singer Robert Plant, bassist John Paul Jones, and drummer John Bonham. The band is considered the progenitor of heavy metal and a distinctive form of blues-rock on steroids. Robert Plant once said, "It's sort of a feeling of power onstage. It's really the ability to make people smile, or just to turn them one way or another for that duration of time, and for it to have some effect later on. I don't really think it's power...it's the goodness." For many, hearing the name "Led Zeppelin" or the words "Stairway To Heaven" or "The Song Remains The Same" engenders predictable and valuable consumer purchase behavior in the language of *needs arousal and desire to purchase, right now.*

In our business-to-consumer (B2C) sales and marketing world, "the selling thread also remains the same" in consumer buying behavior marked by these simple five steps: need arousal, information search, juxtaposed evaluation, purchase decision, and post-purchase behavior. These revenue harbingers and the old push-and-pull supply chain management designed for profitable results also remains the same, regardless of changing media, enhanced social engineering, ambient advertising initiatives, or editorial engagements.

The difference, today, in creating product demand , motivating actual buying activity, is the global size and the speed of the conversation platform. The real change is that today, in front of tens of millions of web squatters, your brand is no longer the host at the buying party. In fact, the party is not about buying, it's about listening and exchanging opinions. It's about what Robert Plant professes in the paragraph above. As the great Henry David Thoreau once said: "Goodness is the only investment that never fails," an apt complement to Mr. Plant's words. Today consumer goodness rides high, promoted through opinions of friends, colleagues, editors, and neighbors, as opposed to the carefully disguised, gilded, and crafted language of paid advertisements.

And now a word from our social engineering polymath: "Over 500 million global consumers are active on Facebook; 350 million consumers read blogs, while another 200 million are actual bloggers themselves. YouTube claims more than 150 million viewers a month."

The push of B2C advertising and marketing has Internet-morphed into the pull of B2-Me social engineering. Whether we acknowledge it or not, today is all about "Me, the consumer." This is why conventional advertising programs are doomed. Trying to outspend your biggest competitors is a modern day, biblical-scale sales and marketing disaster. Today, the smartest marketers have the pulse, their market push and pull, and their corresponding consumers at their fingertips, on mobile and desktop screens through their ubiquitous "war rooms," with quick and effective

Twitter searches. The best part of this consumer "goodness" is that you can easily influence millions of consumers to act as your marketing engine, free of charge. They will even create awesome videos and write creative dialogues for the cause. As I have said for over a decade, "The Internet is Darwin on speed, and it's your best competitive weapon of choice as long as you demand it, and as long as you can command it."

Social engineering is all about instant multimodal consumer relationships, as opposed to the classic one-way, sluggish push-advertising that our moms and dads always avoided. Social media "goodness" comes in various flavors, each having a distinct purpose and scope for brand and product marketers. These flavors include blogs (Gen One Ventures), micro blogs (Twitter), social networks (Facebook, LinkedIn, Plaxo), media sharing and caring sights (YouTube, Flickr), social bookmarking and voting sites (Digg, Reddit), product review sites (Yelp, CNET), geo-demographic and subject-matter forums, and various virtual worlds like Second Life.

Goodness, global goodness through the commanding veins of social media, is the great equalizer. Remember his prophetic words from way back in the '70s, "It's really the ability to make people smile, or just to turn them one way or another for that duration of time, and for it to have some effect later on." This is exactly what the best sales executives and marketers pine and fight for every day.

Big brands and corresponding products can clearly be out-muscled and outsmarted without huge investments, through high-performance, socially engineered blenders. Remember, your customers and your competitors' customers are already highly engaged in social networking, with or without you. The real question is whether you will allow your advertising and "marketing push songs" to "remain the same" while your competition is singing creative and ambient hit social tunes.

Green Reign Leadership believes social media costs are very little, easy to initiate and deploy, and, when navigated correctly, offers enormous and lasting brand and financial impact. Does the song really remain the same? With all due respect, in the new world order of social networking and engineering, it is still about the goodness, but it's also very much about the new B2-Me internet muscle of smart, competitive power.

Robert Plant was kind and generous to sign my cherished Led Zeppelin record album cover: "to peter... song remain the same?"

16

GREEN REIGN'S RULE OF NINE

The goal is to defray the cost of time-based competition with or without the benefit of product differentiation.

Peter Weedfald

As you read Green Reign thoughts regarding the rule of nine, think about the music industry. Many magical and heartfelt artists have magically blended various brands and music products into formidable and profitable competitive forces. Yet so many music artists and product marketers have failed. They want to be market makers, but "they know not how" in such a speedy, fierce, rough-and-tumble, highly competitive market. They do not understand just how to navigate and articulate their musical dream weaving into valuable consumer demanded content.

Simply said, your newly inked sales forecast in music, consumer electronics, or in any other highly competitive market is already sweating bullets. Expectations for delivering profitable results in revenue, profit, and market gains stretch "realistic" evaluations to the limit. Your product is a new or second-chance entry into a very mature marketplace dominated by Goliath-in-stature products and brands. The giants have already built deep brand and product relationships with millions of consumers and hundreds of merchants. Your competitors are already able to garner a few extra pennies for their shiny and formidable brands, and have enlisted social media's power to decide the pulling fate of other products juxtaposed on the shelf. They have the power to scotch competitors through almost instant calculated price swings.

So, your product offense must overcome years of effective selling, advertising, marketing, consumer use, shelf space, brand-to-price value erosions, editorial reviews, and big social-media interactions. We do not sell in a vacuum. Yes, expressing valued product differentiation to both consumers and merchants to muscle up your price in relation to product value, forecasted profit, and assorted line logic is clearly a Herculean task. If you are in a hyper-changing, short product-life-cycle market (consumer electronics), you have even more pressure. We call this market environment "time to volume", as your bell curve product profit cycles naturally accelerate, demanding fast volume as soon as you break out of the gate, as new products inevitability enter and sell fast in your category, at lower prices, with technology enhancements. If your supply rhythm falters in the first ninety days, you will wind up adding a new exhibit to the museum of failed products.

Beyond the obvious need to drive a dauntless product business plan addressing both market dynamics and opportunity, there is more. You must target best buyer communities and competitive products, focusing on features, advantages, benefits, and price points. You must develop product offense action plans to ensure success. So, Green Reign Leadership kindly offers the rule of nine: nine true marketing and advertising tips to support your volume forecast umbrella, serve as a foundation for greater results, and helps to defer the cost of time-based competitors in the music business, in any business:

1. **Shocking yet silly news:** research has determined that a multitude of consumers remember your commercial or your ad, but cannot remember your brand or product offering. Just think about TV or online ads/commercials you saw on in the past few days. Did you reach the same conclusion about them? If you are more interested in selling than in entertaining consumers or delivering your product's facts not your product's metaphors, and if you want a successful time-to-volume business, then amplify and expose your brand's identity and competitive product value in any communication. Consumers want the product knowledge to best understand and respect your product's competitive value.

2. **Your brand and product are your profit heroes;** *a twisting advertising metaphor is not your hero.* Metaphoric, long, drawn-out stories in short clips, concluding with feeble snapshots of brand product continue to amaze me. As you travel through the last three feet of the sale, there are no rocket ships and no dancing bears in the aisle. Profit from your brand and product, profit from your heroes!

3. **Show us the package;** *we'll show you the money.* At the last three feet of the sale your goal is to connect your marketing and advertising to your packaging, and to the cash register. Advertising that displays your packaging is a much more effective sales catalyst than ads that do not. Your package is your most important selling image both in advertising and highly competitive retail shelves.

4. **Open with impact.** Your goal in five to thirty seconds of any advertisement is to gain the attention, interest, conviction, desire, and sale closing commitment of a consumer to purchase your product or brand. This is a mammoth, competitive, critical task. For example, when you advertise fire extinguishers, open up with a blazing fire, then let your brand and product be the consumers' hero.

5. **When you have something to say;** sing it, and *sing it loud and differently.*

6. **Always embrace, serenade,** hug, kiss, and love your product with passion, and determination. So many competitors don't. There are products crying on retail shelves and in advertising spots because their owners don't bother to love them—so consumers just ignore them.

7. **Humanize the object of desire** painted across the cold steel of your P&L. Expose it, close up. The closer you expose a delicious chocolate candy bar to consumers, the more you make people's mouths water, the more they hunger for your chocolate and support your dream of entrancing their palates. Sell the dream of chocolate up close—let your competitors sell the metaphor of chocolate from afar.

8. **Coring down and heaving up drives** return on investment (ROI). Hunt down and secure the right communication locations, and articulate high-impact and highly relevant creative messaging. Then deploy your messaging consistently and frequently in those given mediums. It is better to be an inch deep with the right potential buyers than a mile wide with people who won't become buyers or be satisfied if they do.

9. **Clarity is sometimes a casualty.** The ambiguous, indirect advertising that is fed to consumers continues to amaze me. It almost redirects, "We are in the sales-avoidance business, please do not buy from us." Be crystal clear, be competitively clear. Consumers are busy and their attention is already fatigued; creating demand is expensive.

To hold off competitors, avoid marketing cacophony, muscle up profitability and market share, build rhythmic impact against your competitors, deploy the Green Reign Leadership rule of nine. Even the Beatles knew about the power of this refulgent rule. Remember?

"Number nine, number nine..."

17

PRICING PANDEMONIUM

A friendship founded on business is better than a business founded on friendship.

John D. Rockefeller (1874-1960)

Go ahead and call us price-sensitive consumers, bargain-basement pedestrians, cheeseparing carbon units, or perhaps just a collection of hungry buyers muscling in on the best prices, deals, and selections, trying to enjoy the best of times all the time. After all, we all believe we owe ourselves the very best deals. The reality and importance of commanding and protecting profitable pricing is the lifeblood of opportunity. And of course if managed poorly, the predictable demise of failure.

As a buying society we have dramatically and forever changed and heightened our demands for the lowest price, for all we buy, all the time. But it's not change for change's sake alone.

We changed to personally profit from the mammoth and wide spread surge of low internet product pricing, enabling us to buy the same products and brands we used to purchase solely in more expensive retail stores. This is real-time change that consumers can profit from and are now also benefiting from even while trolling the aisles of retail stores. Green Reign Leadership strives to stay ahead of such change in pricing to ensure continued competitive advantage. It is most important to understand these dynamic price changes to manage the change, before the change manages our business.

The Internet, with the power of always-on push-and-pull connectivity is integrating and aggregating retail store price stickers, retail placards, and the once industry-united manufacturer's suggested retail prices (MSRPs) instantly and effectively through consumer accessed clouds. Generic bar code readers (QR's) on consumer cell phones offer an instant path to direct internet competitors, preventing retail price tags on the floor from declaring best prices. The QR app vacuums in special deals and offers, instantaneously. Consumers have opted-in to thousands of no-name-brand exclusive networks or social groups to receive instant special pricing deals on time, all the time.

In addition, best deals auto-connect to mobile devices, then instantly spread through socially engineered hubs and nodes; these are expansive friend and family empires. Traditional retailers struggle to match skinny, low-overhead "cloud pricing" businesses. Shackled with hefty brick-and-mortar costs, retailers must find another way. Imagine: many internet based stores are releasing cell phone apps allowing mobile users to compare retail store prices by simply scanning the product's barcode, photographing the product, or simply saying its name. "Ouch," for retailers and "Bravo" to smart internet sites and consumers who are pushing and pulling ubiquitous and nanosecond best pricing.

We, as niggling, price-conscious consumers, need to praise smart, smartly pushed and pulled prices delivered through "cash register" clouds. Green Reign Leadership suggests brick and dot-com retailers, as well as brands themselves, are hyper-exploring new sales and product marketing opportunities through this paradigm shift, including:

Group buying: Millions of "ready and able to buy" consumers now exercise their collective buying power through a host of cloud and social networks like Groupon, Living Social, GoNabit, and DailyDeal. Even national retailers use Facebook to run group-buying deal, exceeding thousands of "likes" to make the group deal happen within twenty-four hours.

Flash sales: This is all about historic time-limited offers. Call it the "blue light special in aisle seven." It is really all about instantly dumping excess inventory across the Internet to members, guests, and social networks, all ready to buy instantly. A multitude of companies have earned instant sales and profit success using Twitter or Facebook flash-sales programs. Volume increases through your supply chain deliver much-needed profitability increases. Flash sales provide the key to turning over your product profit engine again and again.

Dynamic pricing: Think Priceline, Orbitz, Travelocity, and hundreds more that recondition standard published prices based on excess inventory, dynamically raising and lowering prices, based on availability and demand.

GEO-demographic selling: With consumers willingly broadcasting their physical locations, brands and retailers can push the deal of the minute virtually at the point of sale. The best at this have a sharp CRM data-mining group feed in highly relevant offers based on age, product, service preferences, and even household incomes. Imagine it is back-to-school time and fourteen-year-old Jenny is walking with mom past a retail store in the shopping mall when an instant message pings Jenny's phone to let her know the hot new Go Go backpack is on sale at 40 percent off for the next ten minutes only twenty feet away from mom's pocketbook.

Membership has its privileges: The traditional club retail format, such as Costco, Sam's Club, and BJ's, has morphed into thriving online niche club communities. Member sales are an earned privilege with many willing to pay for it, either through an e-club card or by sharing personal preferences with purposeful club-buying habits. By the way, Costco and Sam's are leading this charge.

Expect to see and experience more instant e-pricing pandemonium as we mature this mammoth surge to volume sales. It is most important for your company to explore, discover, harness, and deploy your own creative form of competitive pressure pricing applied to launching a new product; to super fuel excess inventory; to subjugate a granite wall competitor; to provide profits to your P&L; and to expose your new products and brands. And in our fluid push-and-pull consumer-centric buying world, rematches are instant, fast, and furious. Trust me, every retailer wants a pricing rematch unfortunately, many want a rematch after it is too late.

18

■DIGITAL CAPITALISM■

He is richest who is content with the least, for content is the wealth of nature.

Socrates (470 – 399 BC)

How fortunate we are to learn from a global gale of creative and innovative risk takers. They are shaking up the relationship of our senses through a multitude of glowing information and entertainment screens in different flavors, sizes, and shapes. The robust electronics business climate, geared to enjoying fresh, competitive technology enhancements, super fuels the great digital divide again and again. This shift creates nail-biting losses for some leaders and wealthy success stories for many others. Welcome to the world of digital capitalism, where consumers just cannot resist another glowing, connected device and where Green Reign leaders need a deeper and richer understanding of the digital tools used to enlist and ensure competitive advantage.

Having said this, hurray for consumers, who benefit so rapidly from a multitude of these devices and who have so much choice in where to buy, physically or through e-clouds, reaping the best prices and return for their personal investments. It is just so hard to resist buying and traveling through that beautiful piece of connected glass!

As we know, consumer demands for low prices have forced the traditional bell curves of product profitability cycles into new time-to-volume, razor-sharp business models, where profits must be accumulated immediately on launch and rearticulated for quicksilver potential in the range of sixty to ninety days. We all agree that the demand to buy electronics is enormous. However, consumers are quick to say "bye, not buy" to any retailer or e-tailor when the buying experience does not pass muster judged against shopping expectations

Of course, to ensure buying success, any e-site's standard bill of fare must be to provide a creatively energizing, enjoyable, and valuable shopping experience, including deals of the day, cool auctions, highly competitive pricing, and group buys. Smart and aggressive e-tailers and retailers dominate their online competitive positions by employing the historic e9 substrate. C-level polymaths already know each e9 lever should be audited monthly for strength or weakness strains with respect to e-sales, marketing forecasts, and profit returns. The Green Reign Leadership e9 levers are:

1. Customer relationship management (CRM), with a highly integrated data mining backend.
2. Search engine optimization (SEO), to ensure the widest, most relevant visibility and ROI performance.
3. Pay for clicks (PFC), designed to core down and heavy up profitability with the best, most relevant and active buyers.
4. Pay for performance (PFP), designed to share reasonable profits with media and distribution partners.
5. Post a blog (PAG), designed to build social and subject interest traffic to click through to your site.
6. Link your site (LYS) spiders, designed to follow links, aggregate various site content, and fuse to search engine databases.

7. Affiliate marketing programs (AMP) builds relevant, profitable terms from pay for leads to pay for customer acquisition.
8. Banner exchange programs (BEP) exchanges fertile, valuable banner placement with complementary sites.
9. Listed in directories (LID) improves your site's traffic and social popularity.

Digital capitalism and market acceleration will increase in ways we cannot even imagine once TV and Internet integration becomes seamless, organic, and ubiquitous. Imagine watching a TV show in your living room and clicking on one of the stars' suit jackets , revealing color availability, buying sites, and an instant "buy in the next ten minutes and receive an extra twenty percent off, no shipping, same day delivery" message. The Green Reign Leadership e9 pillars are designed to change historically measured audience participation into the new digital capitalism language of audience profitability.

Our global technology outlook is long, bright, and exciting. Our ability as consumers to enjoy instant buying gratification using such products and tools to find the best price, at the best time and location is evolving rapidly. Any website's e9 back and front end should always be designed to set up new as well as future boomerang buying behavior. It should be designed to capture and predict consumer behavior, expectations, and measurements. I know that we all wish buying and selling was really simple and easy especially through an irresistible piece of glass. The buying participation of consumers builds digital capitalism through the reigns of your company, through the heart of your strategy to compete.

19

YOU SAY GOOD-
BYE AND I SAY HELLO

Give up what appears to be doubtful for what is certain.

Muhammad Ali (1942 -)

It was in 1967, that the Beatles performed the prescient social networking song "Hello, Goodbye." For three minutes and twenty-four seconds the world stopped and listened to this new hit song, trying to interpret the meaning of the words. Was it as simple as someone brushing you off by saying "Good-bye" while you pushed back and said "Hello?"

Of course, in our modern day, Green Reign Leadership world of sales and marketing chores, these words offer highly relevant meanings. "Hello, hello... I don't know why you say good-bye, I say hello." Perfect. I wonder if consumers forty-four years ago would ever have imagined we would use remote controls to say good-bye to TV commercials and radio spots and that we would hyper-click with our mice on PCs, our fingers on tablets, slates, and mobile phones to say good-bye to old-fashioned, intrusive, and abusive push commercials? We say good-bye by simply deleting, flipping, or skipping through once viable, now seemingly brute tour de forces of nonsensical, metaphoric advertisements. As in those famous Beatles lyrics: "You (the consumer) say stop, and I (the advertiser) say go, go, go: *oh no!*"

What is the point? Well there are two Green Reign Leadership points.

The first point is that I am willing to bet those who read these words cannot remember one TV, radio, or Internet commercial from last night, let alone the day before yesterday. The only exception is remembering a particular Insurance ad (because of the hundreds of millions of dollars the company spends), and perhaps a bunch of other insurance companies trying to catch a ride on their tail.

So the financially focused CEO (Chief Executive Officers), COO (Chief Operating Officers) and CFO (Chief Financial Officer) of major companies constantly ask Green Reign Leadership this question: :"Why don't we remember the advertisements we view on the television? Why do we spend so much money on television advertising if we cannot measure the results in the language of ROI (Return on Investment)? If consumers do not remember the commercials or what we are trying to sell, why are we spending the money to advertise? If consumers are not taking action and purchasing our products, why are we spending money to advertise?"

Mostly, you do not remember because **the advertisements are simply not relevant to you.** The ads do not deliver the product knowledge (features, advantages, and benefits or pricing) you crave as a potential shopper. Instead, the ads are highly metaphoric and attempt to be comical, leaving very smart consumers frustrated, disappointed, and confused. Hence, they flip, flip, and say good-bye through the remote control. In a world where the majority of intelligent shoppers have cell phones, PCs, and other glowing boxes at their fingertips, it continues to amaze me that ad agencies create nonsensical thirty-second spots that focus on twenty-four seconds of a mystery metaphor, leaving only six seconds to reveal the product. That's so broken, useless, and completely opposite of how consumers think and shop. These ads are a waste of time, money, and resources, as well as generate enough failed products to fill a museum with this old-school method of promoting products and services.

The second point is evolution is revolution for those who foresee it and for those who recognize it. For sixty years the history of marketing communications has been about convincing consumers to take action. Today, in order to have consumers say hello when you, the advertiser, says hello, you must recast your push methods, your strategy, and tactics to the new consumer style of engagement. You need to move away from expensive broadcast mediums to narrowcast and micro-cast engagements. These are less expensive, much harder to focus on and much more valuable when accomplished. We have reached a critical inflection moment in our society's evolutionary path, with consumers wresting power and control away from the camp of traditional marketing wisdom. Today, the consumer is the great gate keeper, not the aggressive advertising agency, not your company, pushing old-school advertising methodologies.

Curtis Sliwa, founder of The Guardian Angels with FrancesAnn and Peter Weedfald. I was so honored to receive the Archangel Lifetime Leadership award as well as participate formerly as a Board member for the incredible and global Guardian Angels.

Publishers know this well. I was both fortunate and honored to be a publisher with the Ziff Davis Publishing Company for ten years. I learned from the very best, most innovative and intelligent creators in the industry. We understood that the four towering pillars of successful "new school" publishing were the same pillars for successful advertisers and marketers who were marketing and selling their products. Green Reign Leadership believes to ensure best practice and results in GMROAE (Gross Margin Return On Advertising Expenses) your advertising must:

1. Communicate your brand, products and services often to the most effective audience you seek and the audience you can better serve than your competition.
2. Core down and heavy up; that is, highly focus your marketing investment and messaging resources on your very best buyers first and foremost. And focus on them with big impact, smart relevancy and highly fluid consistency.
3. Deliver relevant and highly valuable content, not metaphoric pap, to those who have the will, need, and means to take action.
4. Understand your potential buyers by acting, selling, and marketing like a publisher. Publishers start with a content strategy designed to target a particular buying audience. They ask these basic questions: Who are my readers? How do I reach them? What are their motivations? What are their content-informational needs? How can I help them? How can I better serve them then my competition can? What content, cosmetics and packaging will compel them to purchase my product and my brand right now? What price points are most relevant and activating for them to purchase my product right now?

The old school of promotion was interruptive push advertising and marketing. Launching a new product especially demanded the purchase of expensive, hard-to-measure-and-quantify advertising, running metaphoric ads, and a push for third-party editorial reviews. The new school focuses on highly relevant engagement advertising and marketing. Consumers want authenticity, not spin; they want peer participation, not ad propaganda; they want personal engagement, not broad push.

Advertising was never supposed to be about ad agencies winning awards; rather it should be about your company winning business. Engagement marketing, socially engineered marketing, is made up of consumer generated blogs, chat rooms, consumer reviews, editorial reviews, and relevant facts, not metaphoric fiction. Engagement drives results and hellos, and discourages good-byes. Clearly in this very open world we live in—shifting, multichannel, web-centric, hyper-changing, with a short product life and pricing cycle—relevant social engagements and open environments work better than intrusive push marketing.

Consumers are drawn to other consumers for product and service information because they feel consumers speak straight and evaluate product features, advantages, and benefits. They offer assurances that they have tried the product and that it is great, poor, or okay. There is a bond and trust in consumer-to-consumer exchanges. Unlike the majority of TV commercials, consumers talk about the product's price, value based on that price and on other products in the same category.

Just imagine if advertisers in 1967 had understood and acted on this straight-information based engagement marketing, as opposed to trying to broadly push consumers around. I've got to believe the title of this epic hit song would have been changed from "Hello, Goodbye" to "Hello, Good-**buy.**"

20

GIVE ME MORE, GIVE ME MORE

Learn from yesterday, live for today, hope for tomorrow.

Albert Einstein (1879 – 1955)

Green Reign Leadership recognizes that there are a multitude of dramatic shifts in our lives as smart products and applications shrink our planet. These products and programs change the way our personal and business worlds engage, and they reconfigure how businesspeople react and interact together. Intelligent hardware and software hidden inside simple, user-friendly devices speeds up our transactions and delivers knowledge (and the power that goes with it) within nanoseconds. They connect us directly and indirectly to our content-filled "cloud-e world" of home, mobile, and business destinations. Every aspect of our lives benefits from smart dashboard instrumentation, global interconnection, and vast software and hardware infusions, on demand. Every aspect of our lives is enveloped and woven around this amazing and seemingly self-supporting Internet matrix.

I define the Internet as "Darwin on speed" because the Internet is clearly the fastest union of push and pull in the entire galaxy. The low-ceiling consumer content clouds, hyper-fast tectonic platforms of varying applications, low-cost data-storage lockers, and fast-paced global traffic routing are changing and enriching our business and personal lives. Instant content transactions that seem to leap from our fingertips to our eyes have become the drug-like fixation of our mobile lifestyles. As the song says, "Yeah...give me more, give me more." Surely the words must be about our instant, content-rich lives.

America: land of the free and home of the brave pioneers of information technology. We fuse software, hardware, and connectivity to create our most valuable and profitable global growth engine architecture. This digital platform allows easy-access applications, easy plug-in architecture, and easy use in global deployment. We lead a burgeoning era of global business growth, based on technology leaders' passionate aspirations to widen and mature smart computing innovations.

From a business perspective, Green Reign Leadership believes it is all about one-to-one and one-on-one customer opportunities. Your goal is to understand customers' behavior patterns and relevant needs better than your competition does. With smart tools we can optimize profitability in real time, all the time. We can triangulate data and foster flexible decision-making to benefit our customers and benefit our own businesses. As we all know, "risk never sleeps." In a word of data from the e-cloud, we can assess risk minute by minute, profit pool by profit pool, reducing deployment times from weeks to minutes. Instant performance measurement has become the standard bill of fare. Hundreds of thousands of cloud applications deliver instant gratification driving our global growth. We now unleash capacity with the push of a "cloud" keystroke.

Let me bring you down from the busy, "cloud-e" skies of business progress to be a bit more specific and focused on an example within the consumer electronics product category. Clearly, consumer electronic products are all about serving consumer imagination. Consumers love to dream from their "business desks." The more consumer electronic products help consumers imagine that they are actually in the movie they are watching, or playing in the game on the screen, the more sales and profits will rise. Guitar Hero is a great example of serving the imagination: any consumer can instantly morph into a virtuoso "guitar hero." No lessons, little practice, perfect pitch, perfect sound, perfect fingers, perfect music, "Yeah...give me more, give me more." Now *that's* serving consumer imagination, which then serves the business P&L beyond the CFO's imagination.

Let us pause to recognize the example of several outstanding consumer electronics category products that are reshaping our business economy, personal lifestyles, and imaginations:

1. Wi-Fi networked appliances can utilize any smart phone to monitor, diagnose, and manage the cooking, washing, and corresponding power consumption and costs within our homes. The next stop will be the ability to download apps to appliances through your cell phone, offering additional features only available in our new connected world. Those apps will offer a multitude of data including suggestions to curtail usage and or re-route power or even how to save money through alternative sources and technologies.

2. Welcome to the living room of "smart TVs." The majority of mid- to high-end HDTVs are now Internet connected (Wi-Fi or wire) with the intrusive Yahoo! TV apps. Most smart TVs are content-ready, loaded with Pandora, Netflix, Facebook, and YouTube. Several internet TVs come with a smart hub platform that competes with varying media centers while integrating attached cloud based storage to the television. Proprietary Internet video on demand (VOD) platforms are being delivered and seeded in many living rooms. This content rich platform also allows for easy connection to unlike electronic devices designed for master – slave control..

3. Nothing serves the imagination better than 3-D HDTVs. The technology kicked off slowly, delayed by the passive and active-shutter glasses debate - a debate that is still alive and well. Consumers demand no 3-D glasses and an even more realistic viewing experience in the coming years before they will adopt current flavors of 3-D televisions. They also need to have pervasive, mainstream 3D content before they will vote extra with their pocketbooks for a new 3D television.

4. Here come the connected and smart car companies. Access to cloud computing, data resources and entertainment content will become main stream on all new vehicles: and a new source of expanded revenue and profits for company providers.

5. Our physical bodies also matter in this new smart electronics world. Fitness apps rain down from millions of content clouds all designed to monitor and improve our health. Digital health, digital fitness, and home and mobile monitoring are all accelerating into our daily lives, racing to catch up with the warranted value of other "smart" electronic devices. Here come wireless sensors to measure and display your blood pressure, heart rate, body mass index, and blood oxygen levels. These apps, along with smart medication reminders, pill dispensers, monitoring tracks to your doctor's office, health compliance and tracking symptoms, help you imagine how much better you might feel if you connect daily to healthy clouds of nutritional and personal care.

The point is that our business and personal worlds are accelerating while our technology is being refined for both competitive advantage and to service our out-of-office imagination. Content pushed through any smart device is king, while the new profit queen of this business is the instant download of pulled content: applets, gaming, widgets, movies, special events, webcasts, etc. In fact, the Internet did it again. The Internet actually morphed the legacy, changed the financial structure and strength of the entire TV hardware business.

Content used to be simply pushed across the air into your living room or den through your television. Your only consumer control was to flip stations, record shows, or turn off the screen entirely with a flick of a finger. But now the TV business mirrors the razor-blade business, or perhaps the printer-ink cartridge business. From the perspective of market growth, razor blades or printer ink cartridge sales represents where all the profit action is. "Give away the printers and the razors to capitalize on mammoth returns in revenue and profit on blades and cartridges."

Now, as we troll through the new Internet economy, the same formula is the new reality for the TV business. As TV prices continue to plummet, brands blur, and private label retail brands are seeded, it is very tough to make a profit just selling TVs. However, the very good news for profits is that the majority of new TVs are Internet ready. The "blades or ink cartridge" profit opportunities for TVs come from the added value of movies, applets, widgets, special events, and gaming downloads.

However, the profit conundrum that exists for TV manufacturers and retailers is whether or not they are part of the TV-to-Internet content ecosystem. If those content developers working hard in the Internet clouds have a free Internet ride into TVs across the world, with no manufacturer or retail costs, no federal or state tax cost tolls, and no competitive profit inhibitors, then TV manufacturers and TV retailers will be cut out of the profit action. This is the highly competitive content-profit farm that already commands in our home, business, and mobile lives and just imagine, we want even more.

Roughly one hundred new tablets and slates were introduced to the market in 2011. Imagine just how many billions of applications and various pay-as-you-go content pools will swim successfully through these devices. Yes, tablets serve as a content-selling machine twenty-four hours a day, changing our business and home lives for eternity. This foreshadows a vast opportunity for those manufacturers and retailers who can adapt to the new and burgeoning

TV "razor-blade" business, as well as a maelstrom of losses for those who can't. What does it mean for you, me, and our families? It is all about an array of energizing content delivered instantly to our homes, businesses, and mobile lives. It's all about benefiting from the multitude of tectonic Internet cloud formations generating revenue and profit opportunity, serving our dreams, demands, and imaginations. Green Reign Leadership says with great vigor and passion, "Yeah…give me more, give me more, give me more!"

21

━━ THE GRANITE WALL ━━

With intense sobriety, I say it's true: we either make ourselves obsolete or our competition will do it for us.

Peter Weedfald (1953 -)

Green Reign Leadership believes if you do not have a competitor, you should consider inventing one. Perhaps you could create a new sub-brand or sub-product designed to compete with your own core offerings. In doing so, you will surely open up a hidden, yet highly viable opportunity for competitive market expansion. From a competitive standpoint remember, only the paranoid, only those worried about daily risk and reward constantly, will survive in business. Paranoia, defined as "baseless or excessive suspicion of the motives of others," is alive and well in corporate America, at least the corporate America that is transcending formidable competitors. Based on this definition, count me in as a card-carrying business "paranoiac," or at least an aspiring leadership trainee.

Achievers, unlike tenderfoots, are usually highly focused, with unyielding energy, passion, and determination. They wear their brightly burnished success on their sleeves. When you ask such brilliant leaders, "Why do you push so hard against the granite wall of competition? Why do you want to win so badly?" Expect this overwhelming answer: "It is the fear of losing that drives my determination to win, to smash down that granite wall."

Talk about an incredible, caring Granite Wall. Peter Weedfald with wonderful Michael Chiklis, appearing as The Thing on the movie set of The Fantastic Four.

So, with this emphasis on consistent competitive focus, and as Green Reign advice for gaining highly successful and profitable market share, I offer eleven tried-and-true rules of engagement, designed to super-fuel your team's ability to compete, defeat, and break through all your competitive granite walls:

1. Study your competitors' advantages to reduce your disadvantages. Study your competitors' disadvantages to formulate and build your advantages.
2. Invest in research, again and again. Believe in, and act on, that research, again and again.
3. Analyze and predict strategic and tactical product options locally and globally.
4. Develop marketing strategies that keenly reflect your competitive position.
5. Evaluate all your competition's significant moves and responses.
6. Remember, only the market leader can play defense: get on the offense.
7. Your best defensive strategy is to attack yourself, not your competition.
8. Study and move swiftly into uncontested areas of opportunity.
9. Always confer with and train your sales and marketing teams together. They must think, act, drive, and compete in unison to succeed.
10. Any market with more than three competitors is aligned for a shake-out. Start the shaking, stop the shaking, or start planning to take them out.
11. Treat your customers as you wish to be treated. Be dauntless and highly focused on customer care, service, support; show passion for their businesses. Your customers should be your most important competitive advantage.

The best way to keep a keen eye on your competitor's leadership camps is to live and breathe their products, brands, and services. Provide monthly budgets for your product management, communications, research, and sales organizations to purchase each new competitive product launched. Provide another budget so that they can also purchase their own products and services.

They will naturally juxtapose these competing products, prices, and services, evaluating your usability, knowledge, and determination to break through "the wall." Meet with your team and have the members present the advantages and disadvantages of your competitors' various brands and products. As I like to say in business, "sharing is caring." When your team members share their highly valuable observations, designed to out-muscle competitors, then this modest product purchase investment will be recognized as a key catalyst for success and a return on investment (ROI).

Green Reign Leadership believes it takes intelligent minds to subjugate formidable competitors, take their market and brand share, and to build lifetime value into your brand, products and services. To earn the competitive advantage, you and your team must ensure the highest degrees of competitive knowledge. These simple "ability to compete, ability to defeat" business rules demand a change in your focus that is well worth the extra effort of stretching your business approach.

The personal and business rewards in becoming the *wall breaker* as opposed to the *wall broken* among your market competitors defines the rhythm of your future, the market opportunity, and company's success. Go ahead, take a big-iron swing and break down that competitive wall.

22

▬▬ STIRRING MORE ▬▬
THAN OUR LEADERSHIP

The art of being wise is the art of knowing what to overlook.

William James (1842–1910)

*T*he Matrix, released in 1999, snuck up on all of us. Trailers and TV commercials had an impact. People were shocked and intrigued both by the unique visuals and by the "mysterious" movie trailers, which gave almost nothing of the story away. A hyper stylish blend of intense action, martial arts mayhem, and a multilayered storyline blew audiences away. No one knew what to expect, yet still they had expectations shattered. ROI was also shattered, of course very profitably. This maverick movie's overall global results were excellence in product and brand discipline and resulting competitive leadership.

Creating *Matrix*-level affinity and demand for your products along with complementary halo brand muscle chores through your advertising is as important to your success as crafting that product's speeds and feeds through R&D efforts. Product marketing chores are commonly known as building perception and awareness designed to build competitive preference, profitable pull at the last three feet (or last three fingers in the case of e-commerce) of the sale. In every hyper-changing consumer empowered market, it now seems more appropriate to label this area of communications "articulating *Matrix*-level demand." And yes of course, social networking mirrored to company-commanded social engineering is yet another determined process to alert, inform, and engage consumers to lean toward your differentiated and preferred brand and competitive product arsenal.

Speaking of building demand, I continue to be surprised that so many companies with "me too" products and weak brand association-affinity overpay for TV advertising's underperformance. Broadcast advertising can be very polluted, ineffective, and expensive based on an obvious lack of consistency and frequency, which is how you build preference for your brands and products over time. Of course we can agree that an ambient marketing approach, meaning inclusive media across impactful mediums with a broadcast TV anchor will redeem better results. Please think of one, two, or three more TV ads you can recall instantly; which of these advertisements built brand or product preference for you? The answer with regards to your TV commercial recall is very, very slim. Are there really uninformed CEOs, COOs and CFOs today that allow a CMO the inconsistency of running twenty to fifty, thirty-second TV ad spots across forty different channels spending big, and receiving small? Hard to believe, even harder to justify when product recall and more importantly results in product sales and or brand affinity are paltry.

So, what's the point? Green Reign Leadership calls on William James (1842–1910) who is often referred to as the father of American psychology. Advertising and marketing is all about engaging and targeting using relevant and impactful consumer psychology. James was an original thinker regarding the disciplines of physiology, psychology, and philosophy.

James suggested that interest and its close relative attention are major components of the epistemology and metaphysics that seep into our minds and considerations. James states in "The Stream of Thought," that a thing, a product is a group of messages "which happen practically or aesthetically to interest us...whatever excites and stimulates our interest is real and important." .

We know based upon William James's writing that we mentally and physically repel what we are not interested in, not familiar with, and not experienced in. Based on this, we each become more specialized. And frankly, that is what we all want and that is how we order and run our lives through relevant specialization and the dignity of knowledge we care about. If you personally notice a TV commercial such as one for *The Matrix* or any medium brand-product announcement relevant to your needs, it will "jump off the page" at you. If it is not a topic you are interested in, you ignore the message, and it instantly fades away. The net, information and messaging differentiates consumers, sets the stage for the smartest advertisers to focus their efforts on their very best, most interested buyers who garner fastest attention, affinity, sales, and lifetime value. And smart differentiation creates a need and demand for more consumer information, creating a magnet to your brand and products. Hence, the undifferentiated consumer, product-brand, and TV commercial all ride together on the train to the largest museum of failed products and brands. Target your best buyers in the most profitable, efficient, and relevant mediums and they will in turn target you and purchase your products, your brand.

To effectively build and measure assiduous competitive business advantage, one product launch at a time and across your brand value building chores, consider utilizing the Green Reign Leadership "Rule of Eight: "

1. First, schedule a meeting with executive management to receive its perspective on the specific role of advertising and methods of ROI evaluation.

2. Develop a clear understanding and team acknowledgement of each product's competitive differentiation of features, advantages, and benefits tied to pricing, time-to-volume "cradle to grave" competitive shelf life and after life.

3. With this stake in the ground, the marketing team needs to build a "brand and product value pool" team with a corresponding weekly workshop of relevant associates from product management, advertising/marketing, communications, dot-com, corporate sales, finance, IT, and operations. The team will work closely together to ensure all consumer and industry touch points work in complimentary and profitable ways.

4. This united cross-departmental focus allows for clarifying and defining the forecasted business goals to ensure equal, muscled-up alignment.

5. Together define a specific set of marketing and advertising objectives to support the overall defined mission.

6. Define and identify the performance metrics for insightful measurement of success. Identify what *could* be measured with what *should* be measured.

7. All of this creates a brand and product "dashboard" that stakeholders can respect, add value to, and measure daily metric performance of.

8. For clarity, the dashboard metrics should include the following:
   - **Business metrics:** unit and dollar sales metrics tracked on a weekly, monthly, and quarterly basis.
   - **Advertising and marketing effectiveness:** communications and creative impact, marketing plans, pricing and profit impacts, lead to conversions and competitive share gains and losses.
   - **Advertising and marketing efficiency metrics:** measuring ROI inclusive to associated asset participation with various advertising, product management, channel partners, and marketing investments.

- **Consumer metrics:** the full measurement of product and brand performance through consumers who have purchased your products.

With this level of united team involvement and the establishment of a real-time, all-the-time marketing asset dashboard, key input and guidance will be accessible to ensure course corrections, ROI evaluations, and critical business decisions are all aligned. In addition, TV broadcast advertising will prove itself worthy only if and when all the variables mentioned above value the expenditure in ROI versus other more cored down, relevant information or entertainment channels that can deliver greater consistency, frequency, and measurable ROI.

William James said it right: "Whatever excites and stimulates our interest is real and important." His words speak to the marketing and advertising language of creativity. But his words also remind us of our determination to deliver exciting and stimulating creative ads to the right audience using the right message with consistency and frequency measured through our formidable dashboard. *The Matrix* movie for example, did just this and continues to do this for so many global consumers.

23

BRAND PRINK OR BRAND LINK?

It's not the size of the dog in the fight; it's the size of the fight in the dog.

Mark Twain (1835–1910)

During my meetings and exchanges with foreign factories outside the United States—those with brave intentions to scout disciplined, profitable opportunities across our fruited plains—people inevitably ask me about brand importance toward garnering success. People ask me "What is the 'Doctrine of Necessity' to ensure success with consumers and retail merchants with respect to brand value, recognition, density, expectations, and profitability?" This level of highly relevant brand questioning is warranted fiduciary reconciliation designed to ensure that the P&L is successfully written in hot black ink, not cold bright red. As I like to say, "questions are the answers," especially in suggesting such an important response in brand benediction to wide-eyed global hunters determined to make a market in a new land of opportunity.

And of course a multitude of highly relevant questions across the product eco-system must be served onto the global planning table. The primary goal is to determine the juxtaposed competitive muscle of their expected product lines inclusive to features, advantage, and benefits (FABs); to cosmetics to supply base availability; to cost of goods sold (COGS) to margins to shelf pricing, to product and price elasticity. And yes, many additional questions regarding market research chores such as consumer preference, targeted demographics, geo-demographics, competitive sets, etc., based on product disciplines, product forecasts towards achieving break even to profitable rhythm are standard in such an important exchange. The resulting, aggregated opus from these questions will deliver the knowledge necessary to augur a profitable brand and product forecast. The final brand question for the factory is: "Do we travel through door A or door B?"

Door A: Do we prink, create, and invest in a newly created brand mantle and stamp for our products' future?

Door B: Do we license, rent, or lease an already formidable brand valued name to super fuel, super draft our intended product shelf and market share? (Brand prink or brand link?)

To be clear, Green Reign Leadership believes either brand pylon portends a hefty, sturdy investment. The cost of going through door A, building a new national brand against the din of existing mature brands in any consumer category, is a herculean profit-busting task at best. As I like to say: "The goal is to defray the cost of time-based competition without the benefit of product differentiation." This is true, of course, unless your products are a global or local anomaly, one of a kind, and have no viable product competitors; you simply have the profitable luxury of standout shelf space and standout results. This is not likely as such scenarios are infrequent and quicksilver in maturing markets. Door B, on the other hand, coupled with products tightly married and mirrored to relevant national brands, cast instant, successful price-to-value propositions. Clearly, there are a few highly valuable brands through door B that consistently offer the deeming push-and-pull power of competitive differentiation, the emotional capital of great tried-and-true brands such as Apple, Rolex, GE, Nike, Trump, Starbucks, Samsung, Verizon, Coca Cola, AT&T, Comcast, and Disney. The formidable ribs of each of these wide and fruitful brand umbrellas offer and expect unique products that stimulate fast and wide consumer and business demand.

So, when it comes to choice through brand door A or door B, there is one more very important empirical consideration for new product marketers: "When it comes to consumer choice at the last three feet of the sale, for those who already believe in your brand, no proof of performance is necessary...for those who do not believe in your brand, no proof is possible." At this point, I believe we should collectively address door B specifically to help stimulate the right decision to either build your own brand or license a mature, highly valuable consumer brand. Let's review together through the Green Reign Leadership **"Nine Rules of Rhythm Impact for Brand Licensing."**

A brand license strategy builds value as follows:

1. It builds brand presence by getting product to market faster with a smaller short- and long-term investment and inventory risk.
2. It gains shelf space and builds a rational channel strategy based on brand competitive value.
3. It gains consumers willing to pay a few more pennies per product sale based on the strength in brand value and recognition.
4. It allows a new product entry immediate competitive advantage through brand recognition and prowess.
5. It opens the eyes and ears of the editorial and analyst community for potential product reviews.
6. It paves the "open road" through the merchant community as an instant, brand viable consumer offering.
7. It offers immediate and long-term asset and capital support from the licensor to ensure mutual success.

8. It delivers an immediate and profitable boundary blur in consumer preference versus the no-name brand in same shelf category.
9. It allows for faster global acceleration and competitive marching into other regions around the world with a mature and valuable brand stamp.

You can surely and clearly decide the branding choice between door A and door B, embellishing the power of a formidable fire-brand versus creating a new brand presence in a market, after a careful review of each and every touch point through the product eco-cycle. As we know, consumers are motivated by choice in any given product category. First and foremost, a product cosmetic, feature set, and price must earn the right to be considered. Licensing and drafting a motivating, energizing brand umbrella for any product may stimulate just enough emotional capital for a product to be firmly pulled off the shelf, rung through the cash register, and brought into the home. Then again, consumer-perceived inequity or equity based on brand strength or weakness is proven and documented over time through product performance and the P&L. This is not about guessing which brand door to choose. Instant brand density and intensity are proven and highly valuable weapons of choice in any market. This choice in brand action and decision course is clearly about which brand the majority of consumers will absolutely prefer and ultimately select. Hence, we buy a nationally recognized brand leader t-shirt that may have the same fabric and coloring, manufactured in the same country as the non branded t-shirt, yet we are always willing to pay $10 more for the titan market brand. Why? Because consumers are convinced that if they buy the robust brand t-shirt they will actually play basketball better than if they buy the no name brand t-shirt. This emotional brand muscle proves that consumers are willing to pay a few extra dollars to experience the brand power expected and warranted through their basketball victory shots.

"Brand prink or brand link?" We can all agree that a multitude of mature brands deliver incredible competitive advantage, consumer value, product trust, and highly profitable global license appeal.

24

RADIO HEADS SHOULD INVEST TO AGGRESS

A pessimist sees the difficulty in every opportunity; an optimist sees the opportunity in every difficulty.

Winston Churchill (1874—1965)

Rock & Roll Hall of Famer radio, television and internet personality Joey Reynolds smiling with Peter Weedfald on New York's WOR radio show. Joey is a kind and wonderful friend of mine, of so many others around the globe.

Based on my opportunity to help support a great friend who's a highly talented and popular radio personality, Joey Reynolds, I did some primary radio research to strengthen my resolve. It is important to reveal and teach Green Reign Leadership recommendations when I address a particular market that needs and wants to reinvent sales and marketing opportunities. By the way, for the record and with respect to Winston Churchill's quote above, Joey Reynolds is the most optimistic and caring business talent I have ever had the pleasure and honor to engage with. The world needs more Joey Reynolds!

I hate to be the "master of the obvious." Instead, I would like to be the voice of opportunity in a changing landscape of media and content consumption. I hope you will agree with my recommendations below to spark growth opportunities for those who own, manage, or lead radio stations.

We are at an accelerating pace of change in content consumption coupled with accelerating sales opportunities across all mediums. Radio stations have an enormous advantage over many other content providers. Unfortunately, they do not know it, and they do not understand it. This opportunity holds true only if radio stations muscle up their current audience "platform" with digital tools and exercise their unique editorial and entertainment content. If they do, then the radio station head can claim to be a true "Green Reign Radio Head."

Fat claim: Only ten years ago, twelve to twenty-four-year-olds used to start their mornings listening to the radio. Why is this important? The past will always augur and deliver the future. The future of terrestrial radio and all the ad dollars it claims are frankly, in trouble, behind the granite wall of changing opportunity. Research discovers the most effective fissure through this hard wall of reduced radio opportunity. It is obviously clear that for radio to gain competitive strength, garner ad dollar opportunities, and build lifetime value for consumers as well as advertisers, the model must change, dramatically.

Fat claim payoff through research: There is a new mixed bag of content demand and corresponding engagements among teens and young adults that has forgotten about the radio. The content consumption change is loud and clear to the unwashed, and an amplification of known trends for the "washed" in the radio business. Yes, the youth and young adults (ages twenty-two to thirty-five) have given up listening in exchange for bimodal, hopscotch, and interactive media. This research supports my fat claim and provides suggestions for my radio friends on how to super fuel the size, scope, and value of their audiences.

Although radio listening currently remains healthy as a percentage of media usage, a number of varying formats have muscled their way onto the scene over the past few years, distracting and disrupting radio's monetary opportunities. Social networking, mp3 players, Internet radio, podcasts, and satellite radio, as well as downloaded apps and widgets abounding across slates and tablets, all command customers in traditional radio markets. Why all this change in media consumption? The easy answer is: personalization, interactive communities, trust in pulled social reviews, and conversations instead of pushed advertising. Internet radio extensions for AM and FM stations must be much more than a simple mirror of their aired content product. It's time for six very pointed and highly relevant Green Reign Leadership recommendations to build and re-build opportunity for radio heads wanting to profit from listener demand:

1. **Terrestrial stations need to quickly** and correctly incorporate the latest digital tools. There are so many: applets, widgets, CRM, multimedia partnerships, audience mining, and far more. These all include optimized social engineering tools to find and capitalize on ambient push-and-pull strategies for radio advertisers , as opposed to the uncompetitive one-way push formats in place today. Clearly, I am not suggesting the simplicity of a website foundation, but a highly competitive digital focus to gain your *unfair* share of audiences and your unfair share of advertising dollars.

2. **Invest, invest, invest.** Invest in platforms, technology, and human capital. Invest in multimedia expertise with digital tools, creative planning, and administration using concentrated push and pull, CRM consumer-mining attributes, competitive research, and self-examination. You should also build out your own digital video studio.

3. **Be cool, relevant, quick, and connected.** Be multimodal to serve audience and advertising demand as one radiant competitive force. Or, as they say, "be gone."

4. **Know the landscape** of digital and technical consumer-centric tools. For example, there are first mobile applications that rewards users for any physical interaction with stores. With their permission (and you need a strategy with mirroring tactics around garnering "permission" from your audience with your advertisers), their GPS is linked to store advertisers who participate and pay. When a consumer

walks by a physical store in the mall, the advertiser sends a text message with special and relevant promotional price offers customized to a man or woman. Imagine the push-to-pull power for a radio station at the leading edge of this mobile connection. Hundreds of new plug-ins for capitalizing on consumers changes the competitive landscape, opportunities and returning advertising investments.

5. **Research, research, assiduously research,** to understand the digital platform and capabilities of each current or potential advertiser. You can't make too large an effort if you have built out the areas listed above. Imagine the competitive value of plugging advertisers into your digital infrastructure while they can also plug your radio assets into their own platform. Game over. Your ad sales people win. You shock and awe your competitors and build lifetime advertisers and digital annuities.

6. **Be multimodal** across all potential content mediums to drive your radio business, yet highly adaptable within each medium, exploring consumer capabilities, value propositions, and content demand.

I have seen and lived through very similar dynamic changes in multiple industries. Train track and engines owners thought they were in the train business, not the transportation business, and they lost as a result. Radio heads need to position themselves in the information, content and entertainment business as we ride into this new century. The core competitive foundation for rational planning, even in the radio business, is to grab content and profit transportation opportunities wherever consumers digest data. Be relevant, digital, and opportunistic using any medium in which content is delivered.

Remember the Green Reign Leadership creed: the best opportunities, even in the radio business lie in facing danger. If they did not, then all of your competitors would already have gone into the digital transportation business. To radio stations heads I say, "Invest, invest, invest in digital transportation, and your advertisers and audience will invest in you."

Go ahead radio executives. Step up to this new world of fastidious and dauntless digital e-tools and become a highly competitive, highly relevant, and aggressive radio head. Green Reign Leadership delivers these recommendations specific to the radio business but can attest, through experience, that these same leadership rules are also highly effective across any advertising medium or publishing model, any small, medium or large businesses.

25

TEN PRINCIPLES TO GIVE BACK

We make a living by what we get. We make a life by what we give.

Winston Churchill (1874–1965)

Like you, I have always had a heart for the innocent, those in need, and those who need our greater attention and support. Shortly after joining Samsung Electronics, I created and introduced a cause marketing idea and business plan to executive management. It was not just a program to offer funds to those in need, but rather an entirely new and unique giving program designed to partner with our most important business customers: our retailers, media partners, and end-user consumers. I call this giving back partnership "The Four Seasons of Hope."

Started in 2002, Samsung's Four Seasons of Hope runs retail and consumer promotions throughout the year that are connected with charities supported by sports and music celebrities. These celebrities are true leaders on and off the playing field, as well as across the concert stage. The original sports partners include Arnold Palmer and the Arnold Palmer Hospital for Women and Children; football's Boomer Esiason and the Boomer Esiason Foundation; basketball's Magic Johnson and The Magic Johnson Foundation; and Joe Torre former coach of the New York Yankees and his Joe Torre Safe at Home Foundation. In addition, Jon Bon Jovi joined The Four Seasons of Hope as the official music of giving and to raise funds for his various giving programs, which attracted other musicians to help support our community causes including Pete Townshend and Roger Daltrey of The Who, Tim McGraw, Faith Hill, and many others. In less than two years, Samsung's Four Seasons of Hope raised more than $2 million. As this giving program continues, well over $15 million will have been raised and donated at the time of this writing.

I continue today to ensure that leadership's greatest focus is delivered through kindness and care for our customers and communities. Regarding The Four Seasons of Hope, I invited and contracted our largest four retail partners to join Samsung Electronics on this exciting and important mission to give back. These original retail partners during our program's maiden voyage were: Best Buy (coupled specifically with Magic Johnson), Sears (united directly with Boomer Esiason), Circuit City (connected with Joe Torre), and CompUSA (with Arnold Palmer). This retail cause paring allowed separate promotional programs to deliver needed funding during four distinct seasons of sports (football, baseball, golf, and basketball); hence the name, "The Four Seasons of Hope."

Pictured together for our Samsung's Four Seasons of Hope fund raising event in New York City are Faith Hill, Tim McGraw, Dan Marino, Boomer Esiason, Joe Torre, Bob Costas, Peter Weedfald, Lesley Visser, former NY Mayor Rudy Giuliani and DJ Oh. Their caring and giving hearts have helped so many in need across our nation and beyond.

In addition, even kind and caring business and political leaders joined to support our Four Seasons of Hope giving program including Mayor Rudy Giuliani, President Bill Clinton, Publisher Steve Forbes and many others.

I will always remember and reflect on this unique giving program that brought together celebrity and retail leaders, and an incredible group of Samsung Electronics team members who insured our success in giving back, often. Thank you Mr. DJ Oh, for your trust and outstanding leadership to allow me to create and mature such an important foundation to give back to the communities in which we did business in. And thank you Sonia Chang, for your tireless efforts and caring heart to ensure our united, long term success. Thank you SH Lim for your unyielding support and kinetic determination for a world-class program designed to aid those in need. And thank you to so many Samsung Electronics team members especially Mike Palazzolo, who stood with me and for us contributing big in mind, spirit, and action each and every day.

Green Reign Leadership believes "hope is not a strategy." Hoping those in need will receive the care and funding they must have is not a strategy. A leadership strategy is to create a vision, to sell that story and potential opportunity to others who then enlist their support, minds, and hearts to ensure the best possible results, daily. In essence, leadership is your most potent strategy.

Pictured at a Samsung's Four Season of Hope fund raising dinner in New York City are (left to right): Magic Johnson, Arnold Palmer, DJ Oh, Jon Bon Jovi, Peter Weedfald, Wayne Gretsky and Joe Torre. God bless these wonderful, caring men.

So with this reflection on just one of many programs I have been honored to incept, create and lead to raise funds for those in need, I deliver:

Green Reign Leadership's "Ten Principles To Give Back."

1. **Hope is not a strategy.** Hoping those in need will magically save themselves from affliction, or that they will find the way on the lonely and foggy road to salvation, is not a strategy. Hope needs a plan—a strategy. Developing that strategy requires that you have vision, moral courage, and a heart for the innocent and that you actively demonstrate these. Together with our team members, friends, colleagues, corporations, and institutions we are proud to give back to the communities we do business with, around the globe. We are proud to give back to the communities we do business with around the globe. Below are some photos from various fund-raising events to give you an idea of our leadership determination to give back to those in need. I bet you will recognize many of these kind and generous people and will enjoy the spirit of giving expressed throughout these photos:

When I first approached Jon Bon Jovi back in 2004 to join the Four Seasons of Hope, he slowly revealed his enormous, caring heart.

Peter Weedfald thanks Jon Bon Jovi for his generous partnership and contributions in song, heart and personal support to help raise needed funds for so many in need.

I created Samsung's Four Seasons of Hope just a month after our country's 9/11 tragedy, and the organization came to maturity thanks to the support of incredibly caring Samsung team members focused on *helping children in need*, along with major retail partner's and sports and music superstars.

In 2005, Jon joined as the "official music of The Four Seasons of Hope." He has performed for our cause across the country, helping us raise millions of dollars for children and others in need. His spirit of generosity mirrors his talent, creativity, and rock-and-roll leadership. As I've said, "Creativity allows you to escape the rusty and tiring predictable. Creativity is your most important tool in business to enhance your product, service, and brand value, and make them enticing." In finding ways to give back to our communities, it is best to collaborate with caring superstars to unite creativity, light up venues, and tap into emotions, all designed to encourage participation and stimulate contributions. Over time, I discovered our highly creative Jon is steadfast and determined in caring for others. So many people are grateful to him for lending his voice, guitar, and heart.

Jon's band, Bon Jovi, has sold more than 100 million albums worldwide. In the history of the music business, only a small pool of less than twenty artists have ever achieved such a global mark. Jon proves each and every day what a global superstar with a caring heart can do, will do, and does do to give back to so many in so many special ways.

I will always be humbled by Jon's great heart. Like so many of my friends and colleagues I admit to being a Philomath: I love learning. I study the many talented and generous people whom I get to work with. I learn important lessons every day. I learned so much from Jon, from both close-up and far away. The leadership, creativity, and discipline he shows in his work and his giving are the key ingredients for any brand or product building chores, just as they are for giving back to our communities. Having a "heart for the innocent" begins our progress toward raising funds, establishing creative engagements, and sharing the music of great brands, products, and musicians.

Finally, "Nothing can deflect a caring heart, nothing can prevent creative aspirations from sharing their part; nothing can be better than Jon Bon Jovi sharing his creative music and generous heart."

Phil Schoonover, New York Fire Commissioner Nicholas Scoppetta, Mayor Rudy Giuliani and Peter Weedfald celebrating a $100,000 firedog giving donation to the National Law Enforcement and Firefighters Children's Foundation.

2. **Never let your mind battle your heart.** In business, in giving back, in caring for others through moral courage, the most successful leaders command, orchestrate, and provide disciplined separation of heart and mind to accomplish mighty things. It is difficult to ignore the greater strength of mind over matter versus emotional capital over heart. The mind must focus on the strategy, vision, and the possible in garnering real financial results in either fund-raising efforts or through the P&L. Once the very good financial deed is accomplished, and the administration for receiving and giving is fluid and complete, the heart then is welcome to jump in, enjoy the spoils of giving to others, and relish the emotional capital of smiles, the energy, passion

and gratefulness for kind deeds, giving back with dignity and pride through the community.

Remember, your giving and caring badge of courage has both a numerator and denominator, comprising heart and mind. It is the potential division of this mighty equation that delivers only a fraction of the results needed to stamp out the disease, stop the infliction, cure the sick, and protect the innocent. When the heart and mind separate their missions into unique, yet complimentary forces of courage and support all in need, all in business succeed. "'Give more' says the heart, 'Create a path to deliver more,' says the mind." Together the heart and mind bear the moral authority to deliver on the promise of giving.

Wonderful, dynamic and caring heart Tony Danza partnered with Peter Weedfald to raise awareness and one million dollars in Samsung technology funding to help schools and children across America through an educational giving program I helped to incept, create and mature titled, Hope For Education.

3. **It's not what you say, it's what you stand for.** Words on a tele-prompter: perhaps you wrote the words, perhaps another wrote the words for you. It doesn't really matter; the smart audience will determine if your words match your deeds. Those who have the unbridled thrill to lead and deliver in business, who raise needed funds to care for others, who donate their time and sagacity to help those in need are true Green Reign leaders in motion. Declaring you have a beautiful and caring heart for the innocent is a mammoth public and private responsibility. I greatly admire so many, young and old, who work endlessly, tirelessly, and many times quietly to help others, and give back to the less fortunate, to those in need locally and globally. Green Reign anoints these leaders as "quiet giants," saviors for so many in need. Surely action speaks louder than words. After all, it is not your words that protect or cure. It is not your hope that saves a life. It is your determination, commitment, command, and action that delivers on the promise, turning hope into personal and community reward.

4. **Don't get caught between stress and humiliation.** Many leaders describe how they manage stress in various ways. Green Reign suggests there is no such experience, affliction, expectation, or fear of personal stress. Stress is a state of weakened discipline, a state of declining personal value to a given subject or responsibility. It is a juxtaposed measurement versus respected leaders with glowing kinetic success in a given field. Webster's Dictionary's definition of the word "stress" is most relevant for review: *7. physiology—a specific response by the body to a stimulus as in fear or pain; disturbing or interfering with the normal physiological equilibrium of an organism.* Now add humiliation to stress as also defined by Webster's dictionary as: *2. the state or feeling of being humiliated; mortification.*

Imagine being caught between stress and humiliation: think fear and pain meet mental mortification. As we explore ways to give back and have a heart for the innocent, it is clear as leaders we need to avoid these two deafening and deliberating pain points. Those who need our help, support, strong minds, and robust hearts in many cases live through stress and humiliation. As Green Reign leaders, we deflect and deflate stress and humiliation by staying ahead of the opportunity curve and studying smartly to become subject matter experts. Hence in giving, it is not always financial support that matters most. It is also an opportunity to share logic, and the path to self-confidence, self-reliance, and self-security without stress and humiliation. The inveterate and painful fear, uncertainty, and doubt (FUD) at the intersection of stress and humiliation can only be cured with a construct of logic and mirroring knowledge based upon the relevant condition of the conflicted.

Peter Weedfald and Samsung Electronics partners with former NFL Dallas Cowboys and Hall of Fame quarterback Troy Aikman and friends to raise needed funds for the NFL Tech For Kids program for the Detroit Lions Academy. Thank you mighty wonderful Troy!

5. **Ride the turnpike of truth.** Our Green Reign largess, determination, and actions to help others are a blessed, heartfelt gift realized through our emotional return on investment. The truth of community giving is realized across a toll-free turnpike of slow, medium, and fast-lane supporters. Some donate money and assets; some donate time and determination, some focus full time on the turnpike of truth across a multitude of local and global toll roads. Business leaders' daily responsibilities must include a true giving lane, perhaps an entire giving highway to ensure the company's actions, mind, and heart unite to give back to the communities where you do business. Community development begets, and can frankly define, a united business family of like minds, hearts, and positive and united actions. Start your engines, navigate into a giving lane, and accelerate your team behind caring steering wheels as you competitively super fuel your business results.

6. **Be the pilot for the storm.** The following motivating quotes highlight the giving back principles of Green Reign Leadership . These wordsmiths and "pilots" of charity and giving, who also traveled through storms of hope and need, set the example. They offer us a moment of reflection, stimulate our thinking, and motivate our intentions to always give back:

"The unfortunate need people who will be kind to them; the prosperous need people to be kind to." Aristotle

"It is heaven on earth to have a man's mind move in charity, rest in providence and turn upon the poles of truth." Francis Bacon

"People that trust wholly to others' charity and without industry of their own, will always be poor." William J. Temple

"Charity is injurious unless it helps the recipient to become independent of it." John D. Rockefeller Jr.

The great golfing legend Arnold Palmer with Peter Weedfald at the Bay Hill Club & Lodge in Florida. I was very honored to support and help raise over one million dollars for the Arnold Palmer Children's Hospital along with Samsung Electronics. God bless Arnold and his entire team for all they do for the children.

7. **Know the doctrine of necessity.** It is the standard bill of fare in business to thrive and strive as one team to gain greater success, greater rewards, and higher achievements. The heart, though, also needs, wants, and hunts for the necessary, "the personal doctrine of necessity," to achieve greatness based on charitable deeds. An individual can achieve success by first understanding what support, help, and charity drives personal rewards today and for years to come. Our significance should not be tied solely to financial accomplishments, but rather to what we wish to attain in giving back, in any way, to any need that matches our time, energy, and financial possibilities.

I was so pleased to help raise with Samsung Electronics over one million dollars for the Boomer Esiason Foundation for Cystic Fibrosis. I was also honored to be a board member of BEF. Boomer Esiason pictured with FrancesAnn and Peter Weedfald. God bless Boomer for his incredible efforts to find the cure.

8. **Connect with the courage of your conscience.** Whatever you do and achieve for others in need, and whatever you do quietly without ostentation and without others observing your good deeds and intentions, is most praiseworthy. To connect the heart and mind, to transform mind to heart and heart to mind, brings personal joy for the achievers who give back in both small and formidable ways. The courage of one's conviction to help others is rooted in the understanding that man or woman needs to satisfy conscience through giving, not taking. The blessing and obvious truth is not that man has the courage to own and merit

a conscience, but rather the courage of the conscience owns and merits the man.

I was very proud to be inspired to incept, create and mature a special giving program for our wonderful and caring firefighters across America with Circuit City. God bless all our wonderful and heartfelt firefighters and police officers.

9. **Givers are opportunity obsessed.** Opportunities to give back do not come stamped with standard weights that measure value. The very best opportunities to give can challenge good hearts, fog up clear minds, and disrupt brave intentions based on the heartfelt desire to help, without the roadmap to succeed. Praise those who are obsessed to help and cure, and trust those with good intentions who seek to engage and add personal value, beyond

just financial results. Help and inspire those with good intentions who have difficulty in recognizing opportunity. Herald the opportunity-obsessed who recognize and create opportunities from another's difficulty.

We were honored and blessed to create and mature a special leadership program helping to raise over $500,000 for firefighters across America. The Circuit City giving program delivered $141,402 to the top wining fire department pictured, the Chickahomny Volunteer Fire Department in Virginia.

10. **Organizational leadership creates a future of giving.** The greatest assets in giving are well-crafted, organized leadership; corresponding unity; creative vision; and keen, unending focus. Organizational excellence ensures profitable giving will last for lifetimes to come. Organizational leadership attracts strength, determination, and expectations to

succeed. It is important to reveal the level of organizational leadership structure to potential donors, partners, corporations, and giving investors. Just as concealed talent has no reputation or competitive value, concealed organizational leadership hinders the collective opportunity from exceeding expectations. Unshackle and unleash the excellent leadership audit of your organization to ensure dramatic results in giving to those in need.

Peter Weedfald and Magic Johnson worked together with Best Buy and Samsung Electronics to raise over one million dollars for the Magic Johnson Foundation. A true honor and pleasure for me to stand and support this great on and off the playing field heartfelt leader.

26

GREEN REIGN
RULES OF LEADERSHIP

We have the right, we have the fight, and we will build the might in all we say, in all we do.

Peter Weedfald (1953 -)

When you develop the art of entrepreneurial leadership, experience indicates that a combination of best practices, creative inspirations, team collaboration, and mutually focused goals will garner success, potentially on a global scale. The following eight rules of Green Reign Leadership and entrepreneurship fine-tune and galvanize the many key points of this book. Consider this chapter as an easy one-stop shop to ensure that you gain Green Reign Leadership's greatest strengths and results.

1. **Depend on business judgment.** You must rely on real-world business judgment twenty-four hours a day to be a leading entrepreneur. Business judgment is based on your ability to judge the nature of a situation, the best offer, and the

available opportunity. Business judgment is also key when you create a solution or tap into a galvanized opportunity. Superior business judgment demands that you park your ego at the door and make decisions based on the facts, not on your emotions.

2. **Use critical thinking.** You must possess the power of critical thinking to stare down a profit and loss statement. If you think you can do this—prove it to yourself. Be a subject matter expert, and use critical thinking to make business and life decisions that will give you the will, the means, and the need to be successful.

3. **Face sales motivation smack down.** In martial arts, you need to be a triple black belt regardless of your function or immediate responsibilities. In business, you must look at all of life as a sale. In the next hour, minute, or day, someone will try to sell you something. They'll sell to you—or you'll sell to them. I studied selling on the worst and best streets of Manhattan. Many times, I had heavy city doors slammed in my face along this rough-and-tumble road. I went to St. Bart's Church in the heart of New York City between sales calls to pray to God for strength and determination to knock on one more door. I got my ego slammed, my pocketbook emptied, and my morale crushed—and, frankly, I am very proud of it. I now have tough skin and top-notch listening skills, and I am always motivated. If you are not motivated to sell, then you are not going to make it as a leader or as an entrepreneur. Selling demands what I call "fire in the belly." For those of you who have the fire in the belly, you know your leadership weapon is the explosive drive to sweep the field again and again. You also know that you cannot lease, rent, or fake the fire in the belly. You can't transfer the fire from a person who has it and pour it into your own veins. You either have it or you do not. The mere fact you are reading Green Reign reveals you have this God-given advantage. Ensure you deploy this advantage to improve your personal and team leadership. Remember, you either have it or you don't.

4. **Develop sales comprehension.** It's not good enough to be motivated to sell. You must comprehend how to move the chess pieces around—offense and defense. You must know the best ways to explain your product's particular value or service to your specific potential clients or customers.

5. I have a picture of Albert Einstein hanging in my office with the quote: **"Creativity and imagination are more important than knowledge."** You have got to be creative in ways that are relevant to the market and customers you serve. If you are not creative and do not deploy viable and relevant business imagination, then you can never walk through the door of opportunity and win. I like to say creativity and imagination allow you to escape the predictable. Without imagination you will not excite the room; you will only deliver the standard bill of fare, allowing for zero competitive advantage. Our goal as leaders and entrepreneurs is to serve the imagination and dreams of our own team and of those we sell to.

6. **Give back to the communities where you do business.** Ensure you and your team members have the spirit of generosity to support those in need and in pain. Make sure those who don't have the necessities are given the opportunity to have them because of your sharing and caring leadership. Green Reign leaders know that sacrifice and generosity develop a successful leadership foundation.

Peter Weedfald was honored to receive the Annual Communications Leader Award for the New York International Association of Business Communicators.

7. **Embrace the power of rejection.** Mature and experienced leaders know why the majority of all new salespeople fail in their first year of employment. They cannot handle rejection and failure, over and over. Rejection is painful, and failures can be leadership destructive. Green Reign is about respecting and managing rejection, and about turning rejection into opportunity. We know the word "no" is not a final point of rejection, but rather a "request for more information." Rejection is just one step along the highly competitive path to success, where you reach the victory of closing the sale.

8. **Questions are the answers.** You control the power of entrepreneurial leadership by controlling the question at hand. A good friend who is an attorney says that lawyers are masters of this leadership skill. Doctors, too, remember and observe this golden rule. A doctor will ask you, "Where is your pain?" You reply, "It's in my shoulder." "How did you get this pain and what do you think you need to do to improve your shoulder?" he continues. You answer the multitude of questions and the next thing you know he hands you a prescription and a bill for $122. Ask the right questions to provide the right answers; the right answers will give your leadership and your vision an advantage.

9. **Ensure you are oriented by the facts, not in response to strong emotions.** Leadership involves telling people what they don't want to hear. Calculating factual disadvantages through a reservoir of facts builds highly relevant competitive advantage. Leaders deliver knowledge based on concise facts and details. Leadership is not about guessing, it is not an emotional roller coaster, not a maybe, and not for the faint hearted. A wise and caring leader produces success, based on the facts.

10. **Cherish your customers.** Be a formidable and valuable ally to your customers. Your actions should prove how much your customers matter to you. Customers are not so interested in your pretty brochures. Be a partner, not a vendor. Be a brand arbiter and product guardian for your

customers business, not a supplier. Treat your customers as your mother treated you in your early years: dream about your customer's success. The acronym D-R-E-A-M stands for: desire-relevant-excellence-always-memories. Desire their business, be relevant to their business, deliver excellence to their business, always serve their business, and by doing so you will build up a treasure of long-term memories for you and your own business to draw on, to dream about. **And "treat thy customers the way you would like to be treated, only better!"**

To sum up the Green Reign rules of leadership, you have to know your market, buyers, customers and especially your employees. You need to know your competitors' strengths and weaknesses, and understand the profitable relevancy of the potential opportunity. You need clear and precise key performance indexes (KPIs), and your team needs to own them, believe in them. You need a daily guidance counselor, known as a profit and loss statement (P&L) which reveals gross margins in profit and revenue and reveals your progress toward achievement. The leader and entrepreneur must have a complete and accurate business plan. This plan reveals how to get from here to there, and whether corresponding expenses and agreed-to actions will gain a sustainable profit.

When you embrace the spirit of giving with a heart for the innocent and understand and command the P&L and business plan, then you are well on your way to becoming a great entrepreneur and a formidable business leader. After all, in business and in giving, "sharing is caring." Green Reign Leadership believes if you give as a professional, caring, and smart leader, you will receive profitable results, a highly successful team, and a very grateful company prepared to always stand with you and for you.

27

BRAND INFATUATION OR BRAND EVAPORATION?

Don't be more precise than the subject warrants.

Plato (427 – 347 B.C.)

Question: is your own personal brand, your actionable leadership, highly demanded inside and outside of your company just like a block buster movie? Are you demanded and wanted as much as your company's brand and products flourishing throughout the market? Is your brand highly demanded, company titled and compensated based upon your ability to build brand infatuation for your own personal leadership? Is your personal brand reputation admired? We both know it should be, can be; we both know we all work for it to be, pine for it to be lionized.

Company brand missions focused on revealing and accenting valued attributes, declared target market priorities, competitive juxtaposed strengths and determined metrics should initially focus on strengthening leadership measurements in the school of personal brand development and assessment. Let's title this important personal inventory, self inspecting, self evidencing, evaluation as "mission possible in the language of building brand infatuation." That before you can build and lead a company, a brand, a product, a team, a department, an enterprise, you must first lead yourself, lead your team. After all, your personal brand value will make or break any leadership efforts, commands or directives based on the same numerator and denominator of smart school taught brand and product management. As your company brand is a promise to consumers, your personal brand in essence is a promise to your employees, employers, customers and stock holders. Both brand promises must be as durable as steel, complementary and congener with a gleaming, smart and burnished business heart for your customers and your team members.

To be clear, a brand, as treated in the substrates of conventional marketing wisdom, is the anthem of your company's reputation. As a consumer brand is a measured promise in commerce, a promise revealed, monetized and measured through revenue and market share results, so is your personal brand. And as any product or service for sale should be viewed as the pillars under the company's brand anthem, the pillars under your personal brand anthem will be measured, compared and either monetized through your ability to lead and compete in a market or business recessed and degraded within your core mission to drive demand, drive profitable forecasted results. The latter result is well known as accelerating towards brand evaporation. The net? Brand is a promise, what's yours? Brand is a promise, what's your personal brand worth inside the hallways of your company, as well as through the eyes and ears of your competition?

Green Reign Leadership believes the formidable ribs under your company's anthem leadership umbrella should either reign or shine upon your personal brand reputation. And the pillars of your personal competitive engine is your ability to lead through your vision, your determination, your teachings, your discipline, your team expectations, your measurements and the speed of your course corrections. In point of fact, your company's brand anthem and under pillars should be an absolute reflection of your own personal leadership. As goes the value of your leadership mantle, as goes your company's reputation, your company's future net worth. Let's dig deeper together, let's drill down with a bit more relevant detail on your company's branding chores. As we do, please metaphorically enlist and mirror this information to access, reflect and better understand your own personal brand (anthem) and product (pillar) leadership skills and merits.

Company value demonstrated through deliverable consumer experiences enlists or dissuades exposure for your anthem (brand) and or for your pillars (products), over time. Brand recall relates to the auto retrieval recognition of a brand based on exposure to products within your brands market category. Recognition, based on prompting, is easier to process than direct recall from memory. The competitive advantage of commanding strengthened recognition and recall is vast, especially at the last three feet of the sale in a retail environment where both varying products and brands are juxtaposed as opposed to an advertisement where your brand and products are united as the solitary reveal in a category. In either case, the product itself is constant as the **working hero** while your brand performs and acts as the **emotional hero.** To elevate, promulgate and create emotional brand value, always authorize and drape your product with highly relevant and energizing creative competitive advantage. As brand, in many cases is the refuge of the unsure, product as the object of consumer desire must be anointed and called out as the hero of this dynamic relationship between anthem and pillar, must be over amplified and pumped above the din of competitive brand and product noise. The stronger the hero (product), the more relevant and magnetic the emotional capital for the brand (anthem) will be. Metaphorically, the stronger and more competitively valuable your personal leadership deliverables, the more enlisting and inviting the emotional capital to climb under your leadership umbrella, the more responsibilities, promotions and dollars lean in your direction. Personal leadership that unites and develops refulgent rhythm impact and kinetic results through advantaged anthem and pillar deliverables is leadership that wins time and again building valuable brand infatuation. Leadership that fails competitively, fails through the stated mission, unfolds fast and furious into widely recognized and acknowledged brand evaporation. Evaporation because the team, the executives, the HR department and your customers all wish this particular leadership would simply disappear, evaporate forever.

In either the case of building your company brand or prinking your personal leadership brand, the ability to value attributes and benefits that over satisfy, overwhelm your competition will warrant a positive overall comparative brand attitude. It will also build brand elasticity and desirability translating to steady demand in product preference, product deliverability. The staging for successful competitive brand and product duopoly is the ubiquitous opportunity to build lasting attention, interest, conviction, desire and corresponding sales for your brand X, for product X. To amplify and enlighten this discussion Green Reign Leadership underlines ten proactive, protective and meaningful attributes of building competitive and lasting brand prowess, ensuring life time personal or company brand value. As you read each of these descriptive brand anchors think of brands you personally associate with, you respect and you have purchased over time. Further, as your own brand litmus test, consider whether your personal brand DNA is viewed and appreciated by customers, peers, reports and executives positively through each of these core brand value elements.

In order to ensure lasting brand infatuation, to ensure you will receive a few more pennies versus your competitors brand on the shelf, to ensure you build personal brand infatuation, you and your company's brand experience must be (and frankly your personal brand foundation should be) inclusive to the following 10 reflective Green Reign Leadership brand mettle elements:

1. Personable.
2. Exorable.

3. **Transferable.**
4. **Protectable.**
5. **Adaptable.**
6. **Meaningful.**
7. **Valuable.**
8. **Defendable.**
9. **Affable.**
10. **Memorable.**

Whether you are focused on varnishing your own personal leadership brand or focused on your company's brand and product building chores keep in mind this critical competitive chore is all about meriting and muscling up long term profitable equity. The most formidable and frankly smart report card for your company's brand efforts is: what consumers think about your products, if they only knew about its brand name, only exposed by brand logo characteristics without product. As your competitors branded products are never static, always developing, always enhancing, a formidable and durable brand position both protects your current family of products as well as sustains your buying fans to wait for your next product launch in response to competitive offerings. I respectfully suggest the same moxie formula and examples within apply to your personal business brand building chores and corresponding measurements. Building formidable brand leadership through your own personal actions can also build the same for your company brand and family of products. Brand infatuation begins, accelerates and competitively matures best when in direct congress with personal brand leadership across the sales and marketing organization.

Remember, brand infatuation is a choice, it is a discipline, it is an art form. It is also not for the faint of heart. It is not easy to frequently and consistently deliver personal brand infatuation because if it was, all business leaders and all companies brands and products would be highly successful, be highly demanded. They are not. As an example, many good Hollywood actors and producers with very good intentions have been unfortunately dragged down the maelstrom of brand evaporation despair. I would mention a few for you however, I've forgotten who they are as they have evaporated from my mind and I am sure yours as well.

How about you? Personal brand infatuation or personal brand evaporation the choice and mission possible, is all yours.

28

WHEN ONE IS BETTER THAN TWO

To secure ourselves against defeat lies in our own hands.

SUN TZU (544 B.C. – 496 B.C.)

Success breeds success. Failure also breeds success, if we are smart enough to capitalize on the assets of failure to breed personal and team investments ahead of our future. Vince Lombardi once said "winning is a habit, unfortunately, so is losing." As we know through personal experience, repetition is not the guide post for winning. Missing the same receiver in football through repetition does not breed quarterback advantage, does not signal the teams fertile road to more yards gained. Commanding a released ball that actually spins aggressively and hits the receiver is called successful vision, smart practice, not repetition. Intelligent practice breeds competitive opportunity; competitive advantage. Practice, warrants and garners the issuance of success. Study everything around you, build relevant and competitive muscle memory for every opportunity and treat defeat along the way as nothing more than a learned disability to be respected, to be shed. Practice makes perfect while repetition is simply the refuge of the unsure, of the unguided.

As I like to say, winning is all about ensuring the dignity of knowledge while creativity allows you to escape the sharp teeth of business failure. The three legged stool of competitive leadership and market advantage is built on **practice, knowledge and creativity**. The seat of the stool steadies and defines your personal leadership brand. And as we know, brand is a promise. It is your promise of competitive advantage towards winning in business. And your brand promise is fueled through assiduous practice, crisp business knowledge as a subject matter expert and smart, highly relevant creativity. Think coach, quarterback, team and playbook. The knowledge of opposing team members for next week's game is studied in game videos. Beyond the intense skills of each of your own team members it takes creativity found in coach's play book, matured through intense practice to defeat the opponent ahead, to earn the right for success. Building competitive business advantage is the same. Leadership's promise in the language of this three legged stool, seated by your personal or company brand, is graded through team success, team failures.

As the mirroring formula for football and or any sport - business success is **practice, knowledge and creativity** our confidence and determination levels are competitive assets fueled by preparation. We understand how to practice, we understand how to gather relevant knowledge, but how do we create? And how do we know how to build, mature and amplify creativity? Leaders should teach creativity and imagination in sales and marketing to best prepare their teams to escape and steer around the predictable. The predictable? "We do not need another product in this category on our retail shelves." The predictable? "Consumers are just not voting with their dollars for your product or brand." The predictable? "Your competition has better products, better brand value." The predictable? "We now have the largest museum of failed products in the history of this business." The predictable? "You're fired!"

Peter Weedfald on the big screen arena board presenting Green Reign Leadership principles and corresponding rules of order.

I personally believe it is the responsibility of each and every Chief Marketing Officer to own creativity, to teach creativity, to super fuel the competitive prowess of their teams. To ensure daily **practice**, through the distinct **knowledge** of their corporate brand and market, through the features, advantages and benefits of their products. Most importantly, through **creative** executions designed and tuned for competitive performance. I believe the exact same practice, knowledge and creativity is the responsibility of the sales EVP and all sales team members. And that creativity is the real competitive advantage that allows products and brands to sing and dance across shelf space, to hop into consumer wagons on the way to the cash register and to gain hard fought market share by aggregating sales and marketing as one. In essence, creativity is the chief catalyst for return on investment

(ROI), return on reputation (ROR). I believe the winning formula in business is to have a CMO and EVP of sales as one person, not two people. And for that one person to drive creativity through the energizing veins of united sales and marketing leadership: **to view, calculate, orchestrate and monetize push and pull as one, not as two.** To view creativity in sales and marketing as one, not separated as two. After all, back to my starting metaphor, there is only one quarterback commanding the offense and coaches creative playbook on the playing turf, not two.

The Beatles said it best "all together now... all together now." Sales and marketing creativity: home grown, home sewn, all united and super toned as one entity through sales and marketing. Not two, but rather one. For the "washed," you know those of you in sales and marketing who utilize creativity as your daily best weapon of competitive choice, you will surely call me "the Master of the Obvious." For the unwashed, those who are not primary drivers in either sales or marketing with creativity as your most visible and aggressive weapon of choice, you will most likely call me over stated. For those new, smart and energized sales and marketing leaders, I am sure you are curious and wondrous of just how you can be more creative. You'll ponder "just how do I anoint and teach creativity through the sales and marketing teams and how do I unite two organizations to compete as one?"

"When is one better than two?" Easy, when 2 separate organizations within sales and marketing unite as one muscled up tour de force, one competitive juggernaut, one creative jet stream, one team united to ensure push and pull harmony, profitability while gaining long term market share together, forever. One, in my humble opinion, with respect to sales and marketing, is always better than two. And whether in the game of football or business, if you have two, three or more quarterbacks on the playing offense trust me, you have no quarterback on the playing field, game over. Green Reign Leadership believes and has proven again and again in business that uniting sales and marketing as one leadership team delivers the most valuable and effective competitive advantage.

29

CMO'S & ROI: LIVING ON THE EDGE

Courage is resistance to fear, mastery of fear – not absence of fear.

Mark Twain (1835-1910)

A CMO (Chief Marketing Officer) should be focused on ensuring profitable investments; profitable asset turns towards mirroring projected and promised company growth. My own personal mixed emotions of always living on the edge through my sales and marketing career tells me profit, profit and profit are the expectations of respected and heralded marketing leadership. In a momentary flash I rewind my thoughts to long hours and even longer days through my career as CMO of Viewsonic Corporation, Samsung Electronics and Circuit City Stores. In each of these roles I was privileged to be leading and or partnering the competitive offense in both push and pull (sales and marketing) leading the charge for profitable opportunities. These duopolies in responsibility offered my teams the intended dignity and discipline of push and pull book ends designed to aggregate successful return on investment. In each of these roles I quickly realized and professed the acronym "CMO" really and truthfully stands for "Chief Metric Officer"... hardly ever "Chief Marketing Officer." As you know, in business, it's all about the cold steel of the P&L (profit and loss): it's all about profitable turns: it's all about identifying and hyper-capitalizing on potential profit pools: it's all about competitive advantage warranted by smart, relevant profitable investments. **It's really all about managing and leading "complication, aggravation"... always improving the profitable competitive situation.**

Green Reign Leadership believes Chief Marketing (Metric) Officers also have a perpetual, sometimes uncontrollable situation. The aggravation is sometimes shoved rudely, crudely and unfairly by a CEO, COO or CFO when sales are down, when store or product traffic is weak, when product demand is anemic, when market share is dampened or lost, when return on investment is not obvious, not realized. And sometimes marketing aggravation is more like a sharp twist and yelling carp, more like a whirling dervish or maelstrom of unfair, unqualified, un-quantified charges ignoring truth and justice of the matter: poor early investing in market research, poor product planning, weak product cosmetics, uncompetitive feature sets, too little, too late. In essence, it's not always the wrong ambient marketing plan as charged, it is rather the wrong product developed and delivered by product management, the wrong brand to price proposition, the wrong decision at the genesis of product development perhaps even the wrong sales channel strategy. In point of fact, if the product is competitively wrong then all the expensive attention and demand building both in sales and marketing will simply stuff and snuff the engines of product productivity, brand profitability. Then the cycle of aggravated despair kicks in, product pull fails, products are returned by the channel for credit... yeah, that's right, just another Chief Marketing Officer fully blamed with fault: living on the edge.

So, let's dig in and talk very specifically regarding advertising and marketing ROI. Your ROI calculation should measure incremental revenue generated by the advertising campaign, the gross and net profit margin on the items sold along with marketing enhanced expenses. The advertising campaign measured should be extracted from below the line P&L expenses, not related to channel marketing programs as part of negotiated retail terms. The standard channel delusions and enhancements should also be measured of course however, I highly suggest separately and post related to below the line advertising and marketing pull investments. This alembic separation will best deliver measured and accountable performance within sales and separately within marketing. Of course, the best results will always be garnered by uniting the forces of sales and marketing generators, both focused on pulling product sales, garnering incremental profitability.

Also, to best quantify revenue and profit gains, supposedly generated by the invested advertising campaigns, accounting responses need to be in the language of incremental performance versus current averages, YOY or MOM (year over year or month over month) with respect to heightened ROI. There are two calculations to consider for best review and deep dive assessment to either step on the gas, or tap on the brakes in terms of continuance. Perhaps two measurement slices allow for our best investment examination:

1. *GMROAE* = Gross Margin Return on Advertising Expense

Gross margin or gross profit margin is the difference between production costs excluding overhead, human capital, taxes and sales revenues. Gross margin expresses the greater relationship between gross profits and COGS (cost of goods sold) in essence, measuring how productive each dollar of a company's input cost is utilized to cover operational and overhead expenses. Then we associate the advertising expense as an incremental measurement with respect to net sales gained or lost. The gross margin portion within GMROAE is equated as: Gross Margin = Net Sales – Cost of Goods Sold / Revenue

2. *Simple ROI = Campaign Revenue X Profit Margin / Cost of Advertising*

This simple ROI calculation is designed as a standing incremental campaign performance metric against a mean control and or juxtaposed comparative versus previous campaigns and results. The protracted formula is also useful for metrics of pilot marketing campaigns, A/B splits and varying consumer enhanced sale drive periods. Of course, your CEO and CFO will rightfully suggest all costs associated with running an advertising department including: salaries, benefits, office space, computers, software, share of infrastructure bills (heat, rent, electricity, etc.), plus all of the direct campaign costs must be additives to realize the axiom of advertising ROI. All of those costs added together would give the absolute "cost of campaign" metric to be loaded into this formula. And of course this discussion leads to the CFO's dreaded out sourcing words: "perhaps we could improve our ROI if we out sourced the entire marketing and advertising department." Hmm, back to CMO's living on the edge.

As we know and can agree to, the expectations of advertising, successful *advertising* is to generate kinetic, incremental profit for our business. When we can generate an increasing profit margin over time, we are progressing as expected, we are driving incremental revenue, profit and market share. **When the cost to acquire our next customer is lower than the cost of acquiring our previous customer, we are building a winning strategy, delivering tactical ROI as promised in forecast.**

Green Reign Leadership believes today's global world of ROI (return on investment) advertising measurement and appropriate course corrections is not a role for the faint of heart. Advertising investment measurement returns have become increasingly more complex with the introduction of new digital channels and devices, a whole new host of mobile and social channels plus much more: blah, blah, and blah. Additionally, trying to land your product and or brand message with impact, with consistency, with consumer relevancy, with size, color and determination at the right place, at the right time, to the right target for the right price is a dauntless and fastidious task. Especially if you are marketing high tech products with hyper-changing, short product life cycles. Of course improved measurement standards, techniques and measurable return on investment emanating out of the CMO's office tightens and couples CMOs and CEOs into closer partnerships. And for those who may ponder or wander about, wondering what the eyes and ears of the C-suite of CEO, COO and CFO are focused on regarding below the line advertising metrics, here is a glimpse of the core accountability CMO's must be focused on:

1. **ROI** standard and historic based measurements with conventional, expected bill of fare sales conversions: daily, weekly, monthly and quarterly.
2. All forms of profitable **traffic** generation in-store, on-line, unique visitors, page views, returning or not customers and the short and long view for the size of the prize: the overall basket of sales per instance, per engagement, versus budget. In retail, add revenue and profit per square foot measurements along with basket profitability.
3. **CRM**: a weekly tracking report based upon digital database mining of your best customers revenue and profit performance versus last month, versus last quarter, versus last year. The same trackings with respect to over stimulating targeted customers, those who have proven they have the will, the need and means to purchase based upon past transactions, but have left your business stale, are scant in their visits and transactions.
4. **Customer satisfaction:** Measurement metrics and enhancements feed successful product assortments, selections, pricing and supply chain enhancements. Even more importantly, best in class customer satisfaction delivers best in class customer ROI.

5. **Qualitative and quantitative** metric feedback inclusive to auguring and recommending projected investments based upon data realization relevant to business strategies, forecast targets and company growth goals.
6. **Reveal** on personalization actions and chores, attempts and metrics along with A/B testing techniques and research results for solicitous forward investment.
7. Specific **social-media** platform measurements through such sites as Facebook, Twitter, and LinkedIn are very difficult to quantify with respect to traditional impact touch points and ROI. Qualitative feedback should reveal social media is generally used to build awareness and generate engagement as a supporting role, amplifying other marketing related investments. For example, invested and designed specifically to drive web site traffic.
8. **Mobile** advertising will be important in the future advertising mix however current tracking and measurement is generally hard to ascertain.
9. **E-mail** costs with a keen eye on brand equity enhancements coupled with product, services and support ROI. Meanwhile, e-mail, the mother application of digital marketing, continues to be an urbane ROI asset designed and crafted to retain, stimulate and enhance existing customers while hunting for the next, again and again.
10. **Loyalty programs** especially during heavy promotional and consumer drive period enhancements are designed and tooled for aggressive, long term competitive advantage. Prove it!

And yes, the CFO consistently pulls out black ink on white paper to scribe and report fiduciary measurements in the language of costs, efficiencies, incremental responses in revenue, profit and market share: profitable returns of these costly engagements. Assiduous accountability, core measurements and ROI reporting is the daily breakfast, lunch and dinner for all CMO's, living on the edge.

As we know, increases in product productivity should expectantly deliver increases in company profitability. We also know product acceptance creates over time brand acceptance which crafts the core base of competitive advantage stimulated and advantaged through preferred brand experiences, desired product preferences. Products, in congress with maturing and overvalued brands, enveloped around tuned rhythm impact and pricing advantage is in itself competitive mantle advantage, profitable competitive brand promise. And that promise allows for a few more productive product turns then competitive offerings, allows a product to protract and stretch comparative shelf value, gaining a few extra pennies in price over direct competitors offerings. This is the refulgent language and metrics of accountable return on investment. This is the rough and tumble metrics of all CMO's, 24 hours a day.

Of course, if we listen closely we can hear the prophetic, sometimes demitting words of CEO's and CFO's all over the world as they ask so well: **"Tell me about your advertising ROI situation. Is the complication and aggravation getting to you yet? I want you to know mighty CMO that your last GMROAE results tell me you and your job are surely and clearly living on the edge."**

30

GOOD-BUY OR GOODBYE?

Product depth or product death? The profitable choice is always yours.

Peter Weedfald

L ike you, Green Reign Leadership knows amongst hyper changing short product life cycles is mammoth push and pull opportunity. As we know and experience daily, risk never sleeps. Risk for so many competitors who miscalculate product designs, miss the consumer demand mark based on product cosmetics, uninviting product packaging, disadvantaged FAB's (Features, Advantages & Benefits), weak competitive brand value, off the mark pricing, miss-read market trends, hyped-unrealistic forecasts and poor product demand generation translates on the P&L as dumped, lumped and grumped global museums of failed products: at ten cents on the dollar. With respect and clarity, consistent leadership in the language of smart competitive product development, design and technology advantage is leadership proud and aligned to deliver profitable results.

As an example, the mantra of our consumer electronics industry today is convergence across technologies, products, software, wireless, Omni-connected, internet based: across traditional market disciplines. Profit is no longer solely defined or derived efficiently in product but rather additionally through "d-o-w-n-l-o-a-d-s" of apps, widgets, movies, music, games, etc. Digitalization, miniaturization, low cost glass for access with wireless mobility are driving this dramatic and dauntless change in profit opportunity, change in consumers home, mobile and business lives. Further, intensive predatory competition is leading to commoditization of the industry, pressurizing margins, destroying slow moving product slugs. Manufacturers, frankly our entire industry stands at a technology crossroads. The lucent opportunity fork in the road offers an expensive choice: **"innovate to survive or search for alternative avenues of growth."** Kinetic game changing onslaughts from highly formidable South Korean goliaths and global American technology companies are reshaping the industry demand curve with disruptive, highly consumer demanded innovations. These companies clearly **innovate to grow, innovate to survive.** In contrast, many of the struggling consumer electronics firms are focus shifting, attempting to add new profit pools and shadow portfolios of non consumer electronics products such as green energy products, environmental products, healthcare products, personal care products and infrastructure products for businesses: **clearly alternative avenues for growth.** The net: **hyper changing, demand generating competitive brand and product ascensions cause disruptive and blurring brand and product de-censions. These changes also cause a crises of confidence through corporate hallways, a confluence of factors causing demand for something to change, something to compete with.**

These disruptive and perpetual technology and manufacturer changes are against a widening backdrop of: a global recession, intensified cost competitiveness, technological innovations lead by a few global leaders, internet and applet transparency in product pricing, emerging markets as the key drivers of the consumer electronics industry's potential transformational growth. Profits for the global technology leaders are bountiful while those seeking alternatives for growth are experiencing declining margins, higher channel distribution costs, higher transportation prices due to rising fuel costs, slower inventory turns, faster price erosion, tough love in terms of shelf pull. Also jams up a once proud and fast paced profitable supply chain; slams down future upgrades and new cosmetics, new product advantages. **Commoditization and price disintegration** is causing some technology companies to shift hard to services; support and software: some to alternative products in alternative industries. In all this change is opportunity. And as we know, **the very best opportunities lie in danger;** otherwise everyone would be successful and thriving in the consumer electronics market. But just how did so many major consumer electronics brands arrive to this rough and tumble change opportunity fork in the road? It's all about the pillars of successful pull-through defined as consumer demand, defined as those with the will, the need and the means to vote with their pocket books for your product, your brand: willing to pay a few extra profitable pennies for the experience. Or, it's all about the opposite: no consumer demand, no profit, no future; time to move on to another industry opportunity, time to lower your brand-to-price value in the language of earth scorched pricing, attempting to compete. **The four opportunity or loss pillars caused and experienced by all consumer electronic competitors across retail and internet shelves are:**

GOOD-BUY:

The only real competitive, sustainable advantage in business is your ambient product and brand reputation. The social promise of smart brand and competitive product leadership is each consumers experienced report card aggregating and morphing into either more or less sales opportunities. The daily and hourly goal is to polish the mettle of your performing winner. The metric relationship between brand-product value to price is your great-

est competitive advantage. Now just an engine with promotional advertising and "here come the profits."

TROUBLE:

Entering a new market without brand recognition, without proven push and pull spinning shelf space, without product differentiation-advantage, but hyped by niggling, purse proud price advantage, is difficult at best.

TOUGH LOVE:

You gain shelf space but product turns are nothing more than tombstones in the eyes and pocket books of consumers. In essence, you now have the largest museum of failed products on the planet, on the shelves; you are respectfully in the profit recession business.

GOOD-BYE:

Your forecasts are legitimately and dramatically diminished by the retail and or .com merchant buyer based upon anemic unsustainable failure... your price point continues to fall to try and re-engine pull... **"sorry says the merchant, your brand and product are wasting valuable and profitable shelf space:" And then the dreaded and dream crushing words are spoken: "good-bye!"**

As the former SVP of sales, product marketing and operations for Samsung Electronics and also formerly the SVP, chief marketing officer for Circuit City and CircuitCity.com, I have been privy and schooled from inside the hallways of manufacturing as well as retailing both in store and on line; an honor and privileged experience only a few have enjoyed and benefitted from during their careers. And now as President of Gen One Ventures, a sales and marketing consulting company, I can offer a viewpoint based on tried and true push and pull blocking and tackling through a multitude of profitable win-win retail and channel engagements. As we know, retail shelf space, at least brick and mortar space (as opposed to the endless aisles available on the internet) is a fixed, highly valuable and expensive resource for both retailer and manufacturer. For those manufacturers familiar with just how shelf space product-brand assortments are derived you can easily stand and deliver on the pecuniary relationship between the push onto the shelf and the pull expectations off the shelf with respect to managed turns, margin and forecast metrics, competitive price drops and drive period promotional stimulants. From a merchant buyer's perspective, across the cold steel of the P&L, there are several key shelf management metrics they depend on to best auger potential opportunity, to best ensure a win – win successful, quid quo pro profitable product engagement. These merchant valued shelf model management metrics and corresponding planning views are not for the faint of heart. They are based on tried and true accounting and product marketing practices including fastidious and dauntless reviews. **Best of breed merchants, true retail pantheons are the heart and soul, the profitable engine for both the retail organization as well as for manufacturers engaged and hunting competitively on the shelf.** Just what do professional merchants examine and metric to ensure bi-modal retail and manufacturer success? I offer twelve profit centric touch points for merchant consideration, merchant banking with respect to profitable win-win product-brand-consumer-competitive concords: designed for mutually beneficial competitive jungle shelf space victories:

1. **Shelf space dimensions in the language of space costs, product turn expectations, product profitability (profit per square foot).**
2. **Competitive line logic tied to price and profit margin elasticity and daily throughput especially with respect to consumer drive periods and competing market forces.**
3. **Careful and logical product forecasts tied to productive turns in the language of profitable return on shelf investments.**
4. **Differences tied to line logic between brands-product lines in the language of brand positioning, pricing, item profitability, brand maturity and market demand.**

5. Associated costs for selling, stocking, storing and transportation especially for new untested product categories and or brands.

6. Incorporation of shelf space and cross competitive elasticity among brands in the same category, competing for the same consumer.

7. Careful consideration and understanding of consumer brand loyalty with respect to each and every product sku to best determine pricing and inventory forecasts as well as expected demand to inventory management cycles.

8. Ensured and determined product value to brand value pricing and profit strategies with respect and in congress to in-store and .com competitive product assortments.

9. Solicitous review of all demand generating programs from manufacturers with a keen eye and discipline for all retail advertising touch points to be included and matured weekly.

10. Ensure manufacturers commit to varying and aggressive 12 month drive period advertising – promotional programs with respect to pricing and special product offerings for each tent pole consumer drive time period (i.e. Mother's Day, Back to School, Christmas, etc.) for best, profitable returns.

11. To protect manufacturer margins, ensure retail profit opportunity is based upon stated dollars per product sale, not based as a percentage of product pricing during and through price erosions, competitive price downs and or end of life cycles.

12. Offer highly profitable value add co-op programs to manufacturers to stimulate sales including end cap locations, in-store signage and promotions, social and email marketing programs, Sunday circulars, TV and radio advertising. Ensure these investments are tied into manufacturer's consumer advertising for best results and returns.

Highly professional merchants ensure results through a deeper profit possibility dive: marginal analysis modeling the relationship between a products share of space and its current market share. Clearly, geometric programming to category space allocation with profit maximization is a key multimodal objective across all on and off line shelf space. Other considerations are shelf space responsiveness based upon store location, size of space, competitive throughput or lack of, advertising commitments to ensure traffic and sales pull through. Of course retail is based on the 3 A's: authorization, allocation and advertising: retail is also based upon profitable product engagements think: "increases in productivity deliver increases in shelf space profitability."

Disruptive and perpetual global manufacturing leaders in the consumer electronics marketplace, those who are smartest and can constantly articulate product profitability through advanced, fresh technology on retail and internet shelves will: **continue to thrive; continue to drive their once formidable competitors into other markets, into unrelated market opportunities, into tired museums of failed products and intentions.** "**Product depth or product death?**" Green Reign Leadership believes you should decide through this highly competitive product and brand jungle, after all, you are the mighty consumer: it is always about you, the consumer quickly realizing this shopping experience is either a **"Good-buy"** or simply a **"Good-bye!"**

31

YOU CAN QUOTE ME

You cannot teach a man anything; you can only help him find it within himself.

Galileo (1564 – 1642)

There are so many times in our business lives that we seek an important, relevant quote for a keynote presentation or to simply amplify a point. Green Reign Leadership offers impactful quotes from a variety of global leaders through the centuries. These quotes go beyond clever points of interest or determined reflections for consideration. They offer us insights and knowledge useful through both our business and personal lives. They offer us mammoth knowledge with economy of language, with intelligent flair. We begin with Green Reign Leaderships most favorite quotes followed by quotes from many we all respect, herald and appreciate for their words, their courage and their generous contributions to mankind while they walked this earth.

Green Reign Leadership Favorite Quotes:

- Everything changes but change itself. John F. Kennedy (1917 - 1963)
- Consistency is the last refuge of the unimaginative. Oscar Wilde (1854 -1900)
- The only thing more expensive than education is ignorance. Benjamin Franklin (1706 - 1790)
- I am already ready to learn, although I do not always like being taught. Winston Churchill (1874 - 1965)
- The harder you work, the harder it is to surrender. Vince Lombardi (1917 - 1970)
- Failure is only the opportunity to begin again more intelligently. Henry Ford (1863 - 1947)
- All the darkness in the world can't put out the light of one candle. Confucius (551 - 479 B.C.)
- If you give what you do not need, it isn't giving. Mother Teresa (1910 - 1997)
- There are two times in a man's life when he should not speculate: when he can't afford it and when he can. Mark Twain (1835 - 1910)
- Every man has a right to his opinion, but no man has the right to be wrong in his facts. Bernard M. Baruch (1804 - 1965)

Mark Twain (1835 – 1910)

1. A man cannot be comfortable without his own approval.
2. Allows do right. This will gratify some people and astonish the rest.
3. Courage is resistance to fear, mastery of fear – not absence of fear.
4. Don't go around saying the world owes you a living. The world owes you nothing. It was here first.
5. The man who doesn't read good books has no advantage over the man who can't read them..

6. I am opposed to millionaires, but it would be dangerous to offer me the position.
7. I have never let my schooling interfere with my education.
8. I was seldom able to see an opportunity until it had ceased to be one.
9. It is better to deserve honors and not have them than to have them and not deserve them.
10. The best way to cheer yourself is to try to cheer someone else up.

Peter Weedfald with President Bill Clinton and DJ Oh during a Samsung Electronics fund raising dinner to help support the President's passion and determination to help children and families, globally.

Albert Einstein (1879 – 1955)

1. Imagination is more important than knowledge.
2. If the facts don't fit the theory, change the facts.

3. Reality is merely an illusion, albeit a very persistent one.
4. The only really valuable thing is intuition.
5. A person starts to live when he can live outside himself.
6. Weakness of attitude becomes a weakness of character.
7. Anyone who has never made a mistake has never tried anything new.
8. Peace cannot be kept by force. It can only be achieved by understanding.
9. We can't solve problems by using the same kind of thinking we used when we created them.
10. The important thing is not to stop questioning. Curiosity has its own reason for existing.

Charles Kettering (1876 – 1958)

1. My interest is in the future, because I am going to spend the rest of my life there.
2. Believe and act as if it were impossible to fail.
3. Failures are finger posts on the road to achievement.
4. If you have always done it that way, it's probably wrong.
5. If you want to kill any idea in the world today, get a committee working on it.
6. In America we can say what we think, and even if we can't think, we can say it anyhow.
7. Our imagination is the only limit to what we can hope to have in the future.
8. It's amazing what ordinary people can do if they set out without preconceived notions.
9. The world hates change, yet is the only thing that has brought progress.
10. Thinking is one thing no one has ever been able to tax.

George Bernard Shaw (1856 – 1950)

1. A fashion is nothing but an induced epidemic.

2. A life spent making mistakes is not only more honorable, but more useful than a life spent doing nothing.
3. A lifetime of happiness! No man alive could bear it; it would be hell on earth.
4. Democracy is a device that ensures we shall be governed no better than we deserve.
5. England and America are two countries separated by a common language.
6. Lack of money is the root of all evil.
7. The liar's punishment is not in the least that he is not believed but that he cannot believe anyone else.
8. If history repeats itself, and the unexpected always happens, how incapable must Man be of learning from experience.
9. If all economists were laid end to end, they would not reach a conclusion.
10. Everything happens to everybody sooner or later if there is enough time.

Peter Weedfald is honored to present in New York City with Mayor Bloomberg on several occasions towards raising funds and generous awareness for important and varying giving causes.

Abraham Lincoln (1809 - 1865)

1. Better to remain silent and be thought a fool than to speak out and remove all doubt.
2. Force is all-conquering, but its victories are short-lived.
3. He can compress the most words into the smallest ideas of any man I ever met.
4. I will prepare and some day my chance will come.
5. It has been my experience that folks who have no vices have very few virtues.
6. Most folks are about as happy as they make up their minds to be.
7. Tact is the ability to describe others as they see themselves.
8. Whatever you are, be a good one.
9. When you have got an elephant by the hind leg, and he is trying to run away, its best to let him run.
10. You may deceive all the people part of the time, and part of the people all of the time, but not all of the people all the time.

Eleanor Roosevelt (1884 - 1962)

1. Beautiful young people are accidents of nature, but beautiful old people are works of art.
2. Great minds discuss ideas; Average minds discuss events; Small minds discuss people.
3. Do what you feel in your heart to be right - for you'll be criticized anyway. You'll be damned if you do, and damned if you don't.
4. If someone betrays you once, it's their fault; if they betray you twice, it's your fault.
5. It is not fair to ask of others what you are unwilling to do yourself.
6. No one can make you feel inferior without your consent.
7. People grow through experience if they meet life honestly and courageously. This is how character is built.

8. Learn from mistakes of others. You can't live long enough to make them all yourself.
9. Justice cannot be for one side alone, but must be for both.
10. I think that somehow, we learn who we really are and then live with that decision.

Really generous and a great honor for Boomer Esiason to present me with this special game ball for my work to help stamp out Cystic Fibrosis as a member of his incredible team.

Aristotle (384 BC - 322 BC)

1. Education is the best provision for the journey to old age.
2. Happiness depends on our selves.
3. All virtue is summed up in dealing justly.

4. It is the mark of an educated mind to be able to entertain a thought without accepting it.
5. Pleasure in the job puts perfection in the work.
6. To perceive is to suffer.
7. We are what we repeatedly do. Excellence then, is not an act, but a habit.
8. Misfortune shows those who are not really friends.
9. The aim of art is to represent not the outward appearance of things, but their inward significance.
10. It is in justice that the ordering of society is centered.

Martin Luther King Jr. (1929 - 1968)

1. Faith is taking the first step, even when you don't see the whole staircase.
2. In the end, we will remember not the words of our enemies, but the silence of our friends.
3. Our lives begin to end the day we become silent about things that matter.
4. We must learn to live together as brothers or perish together as fools.
5. When you are right you cannot be too radical; when you are wrong, you cannot be too conservative.
6. Injustice anywhere is a threat to justice everywhere.
7. I submit to you that if a man hasn't discovered something he will die for, he isn't fit to live.
8. Nothing in all the world is more dangerous than sincere ignorance and conscientious stupidity.
9. A nation or civilization that continues to produce soft-minded men purchases its own spiritual death on an installment plan.
10. All men are caught in an inescapable network of mutuality.

Like you, I love dogs. In fact, I care about all animals big and small. I created an idea to give back to those individuals and organizations who help support and care for dogs in need across America. The contest was titled "firedog Across America." The grand prize winner of $60,798 was the wonderful Neuse River Golden Retriever Rescue Foundation.

Benjamin Franklin (1706 - 1790)

1. A slip of the foot you may soon recover, but a slip of the tongue you may never get over.
2. An investment in knowledge always pays the best interest.
3. Anger is never without reason, but seldom a good one.
4. At twenty years of age, will reigns; at thirty the wit; at forty the judgment.
5. Be slow in choosing a friend, slower in changing.

6. Content makes poor men rich; discontentment makes rich men poor.
7. Early to bed and early to rise makes a man healthy, wealthy and wise.
8. Be civil to all; sociable to many; familiar with few; friends to one; enemy to none.
9. Drive thy business or it will drive thee.
10. He that is good for making excuses is seldom good for anything else.

William Shakespeare (1564 - 1616)

1. Excellence is eloquence.
2. Be great in act, as you have been in thought.
3. I am not bound to please you with my answers.
4. I dote on his very absence.
5. I wasted time, and now doth time waste me.
6. In a false quarrel there is no true valor.
7. In time we hate that which we often fear.
8. In peace there's nothing so becomes a man as modest stillness and humility.
9. Strong reasons make strong actions.
10. We know what we are, but not what we may be.

Ronald Reagan (1911 - 2004)

1. Freedom is one of the deepest and noblest aspirations of the human spirit.
2. No arsenal... is so formidable as the will and moral courage of free men and women.
3. The best minds are not in government. If any were, business would hire them away.
4. Don't be afraid to see what you see.
5. No arsenal... is formidable as the will and moral courage of free men and women.

6. Politics is supposed to be the second oldest profession. I have come to realize that it bears a very close resemblance to the first.

7. There are no great limits to growth because there are no limits of human intelligence, imagination, and wonder.

8. To sit back hoping that someday, someway, someone will make things right is to go on feeding the crocodile, hoping he will eat you last – but eat you he will.

9. I don't believe in a government that protects us from ourselves.

10. I know in my heart that man is goof. That what is right will always eventually triumph. And there's purpose and worth to each and every life.

It is my personal lifetime honor to stand with, and for, one of our nations greatest and most caring leaders, New York Mayor Rudy Giuliani.

John F. Kennedy (1917 - 1963)

1. Change is the law of life. And those who look only to the past or present are certain to miss the future.
2. Forgive your enemies, but never forget their names.
3. Let us never negotiate out of fear but let us never fear to negotiate.
4. The time to repair the roof is when the sun is shining.
5. We must use time as a too, not as a crutch.
6. There are risks and costs to a program of action. But they are far less than the long range risks and costs of comfortable inaction.
7. We set sail on this new sea because there is knowledge to be gained.
8. We stand for freedom. That is our conviction for ourselves, that is our only commitment to others.
9. The ancient Greek definition of happiness was the full use of your powers along the lines of excellence.
10. Ask not what your country can do for you, ask what you can do for your country.

Ralph Waldo Emerson (1803 - 1882)

1. Character is higher than intellect... A great soul will be strong to live, as well as to think.
2. Don't be too timid and squeamish about your actions. All life is an experiment. The more experiments you make the better.
3. Don't waste yourself in rejection, nor bark against the bad, but chant the beauty of the good.
4. Every great and commanding moment in the annals of the world is the triumph of some enthusiasm.
5. Every sweet has its sour; every evil its good.
6. Finish each day and be done with it. You have done what you could.
7. He has not learned the lesson of life who does not every day surmount a fear.

8. If I have lost confidence in myself, I have the universe against me.
9. God enters by a private door into every individual.
10. Do not go where the path may lead, go instead where there is no path and leave a trail.

Peter Weedfald and Joey Reynolds standing and delivering on the merits and value proposition of Green Reign Leadership on NBC's All Night with Joey Reynolds television show.

Helen Keller (1880 - 1968)

1. Although the world is full of suffering, it is full also of the overcoming of it.
2. Never bend your head. Hold it high. Look the world straight in the eye.

3. One can never consent to creep when one feels an impulse to soar.
4. Self pity is our worst enemy and if we yield to it, we can never do anything good in the world.
5. The best and most beautiful things in the world cannot be seen or even touched. They must be felt within the heart.
6. When we do the best we can, we never know what miracle is wrought in our life, or in the life of another.
7. The highest result of education is tolerance.
8. Science may have found a cure for most evils; but it has found no remedy for the worst of them all – the apathy of human beings.
9. Security is mostly a superstition. It does not exist in nature. Life is either a daring adventure or nothing.
10. When one door of happiness closes, another opens; but often we look so long at the closed door that we do not see the one which has been opened for us.

Henry David Thoreau (1817 - 1862)

1. Any fool can make a rule, and any fool will mind it.
2. Be true to your wok, your word, and your friend.
3. A man is rich in proportion to the numbers of things he can afford to let alone.
4. Men are born to succeed; not fail.
5. Our life is fritted away by detail. Simplify, simplify.
6. He enjoys true leisure who has time to improve his sold estate.
7. Go confidently in the direction of your dreams! Live the life you've imagined. As you simplify your life, the laws of the universe will be simpler.
8. How vain is it to sit down to write when you have not stood up to live.
9. Do not hire a man who does your work for money, but him who does it for love of it.
10. Live each season as it passes; breathe the air, drink the drink, taste the fruit, and resign yourself to the influences of each.

Confucius (551 BC - 479 BC)

1. Everything has its beauty but not everyone sees it.
2. Forget injuries, never forget kindness.
3. Ignorance is the night of the mind, but a night without moon or star.
4. It does not matter how slow you go so long as you do not stop.
5. Men's natures are alike, it is their habits that carry them far apart.
6. Our greatest glory is not in never falling, but in getting up every time we do.
7. Study the past if you would define the future.
8. By nature, men are nearly alike; by practice, they get to be wide apart.
9. Hold faithfulness and sincerity as first principals.
10. When we see men of a contrary character, we should turn inwards and examine ourselves.

Honored to stand with and meet President and Mrs. Bush regarding ways to give back to those in need across America.

32

ABOUT THE AUTHOR

Do not follow where the path may lead, go instead where there is no path and leave a trail.

Ralph Waldo Emerson (1803 - 1882)

Peter Weedfald has more than twenty-five years experience leading superior global team members focused on over achieving results in sales, product management, advertising, marketing, operations, CRM, Internet commerce, brand building, and Internet assets.

Peter Weedfald is president of Gen One Ventures. The company consults for General Electric (GE) Licensing & Trademark and other companies providing sales, marketing, operations, product management, and retail channel consulting insights across GE Licensing's family of business partners. In July 2008, GE I General Displays and Technologies, a joint venture between GE, and Tatung was formed to architect, sell, market, and support GE HDTVs and other GE consumer electronics product lines globally. As president, Peter headed up all functional operational business areas of the company globally as well as all sales, marketing, advertising, creative, and communications. Website access for Gen One Ventures: www.GenOneVentures.com.

Peter Weedfald has more than twenty-five years' experience leading superior global team members focused on over achieving results in sales, product management, advertising, marketing, operations, CRM, Internet commerce, brand building, and digital—Internet assets.

In 2006, Weedfald served as SVP, chief marketing officer, a section 16 Officer of Circuit City Corporation leading a team of 275 advertising, marketing, and digital professionals. He oversaw all advertising, marketing, corporate research, exhibitions, trade shows, corporate communications, philanthropy, e-commerce (CircuitCity.com), credit card marketing, CRM, customer databases, and all in-store environment functions. He also matured a nationally credited marketing program titled "Firedog Across America," raising nearly $1 million for twenty fire stations across the nation.

From 2001 to 2006, Peter led a team of more than 200 people as SVP of sales and marketing in North America for Samsung Electronics. In addition, Weedfald was one of only 500 global Samsung corporate officers responsible for global planning and decision making, based in Seoul, South Korea. Weedfald oversaw all sales, marketing, product management, advertising, e-commerce, corporate communications, CRM, cause marketing, and business operations for Samsung's North American consumer electronics business. Product lines included: HDTVs, DVDs, digital imaging, home theater systems, mp3 players, home kitchen appliances, set top boxes, and other consumer electronics products. During his entire tenure, Weedfald was also Samsung's chief marketing officer for all advertising and marketing assets for North America. In 2001 Weedfald conceptualized, created, and grew a philanthropy program titled "The Four Seasons of Hope," which raised more than $10 million over six years for children in need across North America and working in legal contract with national retailers Best Buy, Circuit City, Sears, and CompUSA.

From 1998 to 2001, Weedfald was SVP of global marketing and EVP, GMM of Internet Appliances for the ViewSonic Corporation, a worldwide provider of advanced display technology. Weedfald created ViewSonic's "Journey of Hope," which raised nearly a half million dollars for The Starlight Children's Foundation.

Prior to joining ViewSonic, Peter served for ten years in various executive VP, publisher, sales, and marketing positions at Ziff-Davis Publishing, which included executive publishing oversight over publications such as *PC Magazine*, *Computer Shopper*, *MacUser*, and *Windows Sources* magazines and websites.

Peter has directly served, and continues to support, the following national giving funds, helping to raise millions of dollars in the past decade, for these charitable organizations:

- The Guardian Angels
- The Boomer Esiason Foundation for Cystic Fibrosis
- The Arnold Palmer's Children Foundation
- The Magic Johnson Foundation

- The Dan Marino Foundation for Autism
- The Steve Young, Forever Young Foundation
- Joe Torre's Safe at Home Foundation
- Jon Bon Jovi's Robin Hood Foundation
- Pete Townshend and Roger Daltrey Children's Care Foundation
- The NFL Alumni Tech for Kids Fund
- Tim McGraw and Faith Hill Children's Fund
- Wayne Gretzky Hockey for Children In Need Fund
- FireDog Across America with Rudy Giuliani
- New York Giants Coach Coughlin's Blue Jay Fund
- The National Law Enforcement & Firefighters Foundation

My inspiration and determination for Green Reign Leadership as well as my entire business career is strengthened, energized and inspired through the wonderful heart and mind of my dedicated wife, FrancesAnn Weedfald.

62964389R00124

Made in the USA
Columbia, SC
06 July 2019